SANTA BARBARA
ADOBES

SANTA BARBARA ADOBES

by CLARENCE CULLIMORE
Fellow of the American Institute of Architects

Illustrated by Author

ACKNOWLEDGMENT

Much of the material in this book has
previously appeared in a series of articles
by the author in the Santa Barbara News-Press.

FIRST EDITION

With approval of
SANTA BARBARA HISTORICAL SOCIETY

PUBLISHED
by
SANTA BARBARA BOOK PUBLISHING COMPANY

iv

NA
7165
.C8
1948

Printed by
Merchants Printing and Lithographing Co.
Bakersfield, California
U.S.A.

FOREWORD

Becoming acquainted with Santa Barbara's old adobe houses that date to halcyon days has been a fascinating enterprise. Their character varies according to Indian, Spanish and Mexican influences, and most have Yankee earmarks.

In the use of the soil under foot as a building material their builders achieved an honesty of design that fits the landscape and suited well their occupants. Some of these houses—remodeled—still serve as livable and charming homes.

It is well that Santa Barbara's citizens, today, whether they have newly arrived or are deep-rooted in the lovely spot, remember the romance in its background. If this reminder leads to a keener interest in the life and customs of the early Californians, whose Elysium ceased about the time the Yankee horde flooded the land in quest of gold, it will not have been made in vain.

Clarence Cullimore
July 1, 1948
Bakersfield, California

THIS BOOK IS DEDICATED TO

MY WIFE—ROSEMARY THELEN CULLIMORE

TABLE OF CONTENTS

TABLE OF CONTENTS

LIST OF ILLUSTRATIONS

LIST OF ILLUSTRATIONS

SAINT BARBARA

The story is told that Saint Barbara was the daughter of a wealthy Roman and was kept by her father in a tower. When he left one day for a long journey he had a bath house built for her. It was to have two windows. On his return he discovered that his daughter had adopted the Christian religion, and as an outward sign of her conversion had changed the number of windows from two to three, in honor of the Holy Trinity. In his anger the father brought his daughter before the prefect, who condemned her to death. Saint Barbara had hardly given up her soul when the unbelieving father was struck down by lightning.

"Santa Barbara, doncella, libranos del rayo y de la centella."

This little prayer is still spoken by men at sea when a thunderstorm with its accompanying lightning threatens disaster.

SAINT BARBARA

This statue once stood in the Presidio church. It is reputed to be more than two hundred years old.

INTRODUCTION

Using soil as a building material, the padres and the early settlers from Spain effected a quality of architecture particularly suited to the landscape and the people of California. The best architecture seems, in a sense, to grow out of the locality where it is produced. Adobe architecture belongs to the red clay hills and black bottoms of California, for out of such earth has it actually been created.

A study of the historic adobe houses of the Santa Barbara area can not be complete without a consideration of the historic events that shaped the background for architecture in California.

California history may be considered comparable to that of our eastern seaboard. A glance at the map of the United States shows Crescent City, at the northern point of California, to be about parallel to Boston, while San Diego, at California's southern extremity, is in the same latitude as Charleston, South Carolina. California, geographically, comprises an area that might easily include Massachusetts, Pennsylvania, and Virginia, but American historians have associated much more local material and greater historical emphasis with the New England colonies than is found in their treatment of California.

It was actually only fifty years after Columbus discovered America that a Portuguese navigator, Rodriguez Cabrillo sailing under the Spanish Crown, made his way up the coast of California and by virtue of discovery took possession of that land for Spain. Santa Barbara and the Channel Islands off the coast of Santa Barbara are localities especially mentioned by Cabrillo. At about this time a route that was to be followed by the Manila galleons for the next two hundred and fifty years, was established. Since then, California has been under the flags of six nations, which is a general indication of the colorful and changing vicissitudes of a romantic past.

The relationship of England to Spain, under Philip II of Spain, and Queen Elizabeth of England, was none too cordial when, in 1579, Francis Drake sailed his ship, "The Golden Hind," into Drake's Bay, a few miles north of San Francisco Bay, and took that place, which he called New Albion, in the name of England, thereby establishing a hazy claim to California as a part of England. It is of interest to note that the first Protestant church service in California was held by Drake's party.

The "San Carlos," a ship of two hundred tons, sailed from La Paz, Mexico, on January 9, 1769, with sixty-two men. Among them were Captain Vila; Prat, the physician; Costanso, the map-maker, and Pedro Fages with twenty-five Catalan soldiers. On April 29 they arrived at San Diego.

The "San Antonio," which sailed from Cape San Lucas in Baja California on February 15, encountered fewer difficulties and arrived at San Diego before the "San Carlos," on April 11. Juan Perez, formerly a galleon captain, was in command of this ship.

A third ship, the "San Jose," was lost on its way to California.

On March 24 the first overland party from Baja California, left Velicata, north of the Santa Maria Mission. In this expedition were Fernando Rivera y Moncada, Fray Juan Crespi, together with soldiers and Indians. They arrived at San Diego on May 15.

The second overland expedition, which started from Loreto on March 9, was perhaps the most auspicious, as it included the Presidente, Junipero Serra; the Governor, Gaspar de Portola, and Sergeant Ortega. Sergeant Ortega was destined to play a principal role in the establishment of the presidio of Santa Barbara. His descendants are now numbered among the prominent citizens of that city. At Velicata, on May 1, Father Serra paused long enough to establish another, and the most northerly, mission of Baja California.

On July 1, 1769, this party joined the three that had arrived previously at the rendezvous near San Diego Bay. Here the first of a chain of twenty-one California missions, four presidios, and three pueblos, was established. Thus the Spanish empire had its beginning in California. One of the presidios was founded at Santa Barbara in 1782, thereby laying the foundation for that city.

Unforeseen hardships, coupled with the thrill of adventure in the colonization of California, contributed a quality to the life of Spanish pioneers that found expression in the type of dwellings which they built.

No route overland from the interior of Mexico to Alta, California had been established in 1774. It was then that Juan Bautista de Anza, who commanded the presidio at Tubac, Mexico, undertook to find a way. Anza discovered a route for the colonization of California. He occupies a place of distinction as a stalwart pathfinder and forthright pioneer. The difficulties encountered by the Anza party, and the hardships endured before the final success of his colonizing expedition, make the trials of the zealous Pilgrims in the good ship "Mayflower" seem almost trivial by comparison.

At Fort Ross, in 1812, the flag of Russia, or, to be more explicit, the banner of the Russian-American Fur Company, was unfurled. Napoleon's expedition in Russia and also the formulation of the Monroe Doctrine in the United States caused the Russian foothold in California to be short-lived, their settlers withdrawing to Alaska in 1824.

From 1822 to 1846 the flag of Mexico waved over California. The California-Spaniards were never completely won over to Mexican authority, however, and took occasions to show this by their attitudes towards most of the governors who were sent from Mexico.

At Sonoma, in 1846, Fremont and a band of American-Californians hauled down the Mexican flag and hoisted the Bear Flag of California. A few days later, the Stars and Stripes were raised at Monterey, then the capital of California.

In 1848, as a result of the treaty of Guadalupe Hidalgo at the close of the Mexican War, California, Nevada, Utah, New Mexico, Texas, and a part of Colorado, were ceded to the United States. That was the year that Marshall discovered gold, and as a result the population of California increased from 13,000 to 100,000 persons in a year. In 1850 California became a full-fledged state without having passed through a territorial stage..

With this knowledge of historical events that shaped the culture in the new land it is evident that California was a logical setting for the adobe house. But from the beginning, adobe homes of Santa Barbara were something more than mud hovels. They were an outgrowth of the soil, the climate, and the character of the people who built them. It is therefore appropriate to consider this environment.

The climate varies greatly in different sections of California, because of the ten degrees of latitude separating its southern and northern extremities. The Pacific Ocean, with the warm Japanese current, tends to keep the coastal temperature somewhat uniform. In the interior the mountains afford a variety of climates, from the perpetual snow of Mount Whitney in the Sierra Nevada, the highest peak in the United States, exclusive of Alaska, to the desert blasts of the Mojave, and Death Valley, the lowest spot in our land.

Running almost parallel to the ocean, the Coast Range cuts off ocean breezes and causes differences in temperature and humidity in the interior valleys. Although the Spanish had no contact with the Sierra Nevada range, it played a part in regulating the California climate, and later, when gold was discovered, it became a vital factor in the economics and social development of the state.

In contrast with the native Aztec palaces of sumptuous rooms set about exotic patios, that the Spanish found in Mexico, the buildings of the California Indians were particularly primitive. A tepee, partly sunken in the ground, was the most common shelter. In the redwood section along the coast, split shakes of redwood furnished a material from which rude houses were constructed. In the desert the adobe hut served as a partial protection from the heat.

The Indians of the Santa Barbara area were of a higher type than most found in California, although their social organization was simple. The **rancheria** was a town group and consisted of a number of families speaking the same language. The boundaries of their domain were usually well-fixed, thus avoiding disputes with neighboring **rancherias**. The chief was such by virtue of his wealth, influence, or wisdom, and not a king in the hereditary sense. Marriage meant simply the purchase of a wife, social standing depending upon the sum paid.

The charm of Moorish influence came to Mexico, to California, and to the South American countries, along with the Spaniards who were inspired by memories of the picturesque houses of old Spain. One finds, in the fusion of details from Andalusia with California construction, much of the fascination that has received so warm a welcome on our Pacific slopes, not only because Spanish precedent is well-rooted, but also because the environment is similar to that on the shores of the Mediterranean. This is particularly true of the Santa Barbara area. Well-to-do California-Spaniards built about a court, with potted flowers, espaliered plants, and fountain or ornamental well-head, as their ancestors had done in a comparable climate. Low-pitched tile roofs, supported by massive walls, gave a somewhat rugged character, which was occasionally relieved by a touch of decorated tile, or wrought iron in a gateway, balustrade, or window grille. In Cordova and Seville the Spaniards had known the perfection of the patio enclosed on all four sides. In California one side was often left open to take advantage of a view of the ocean, or the mountains, to invite a cooling breeze or permit the **ranchero** to ride his steed directly to his front door stoop.

At first the California mud-walled houses seemed rude, temporary structures; but as they were reconstructed and strengthened to meet the attrition of wind and rain, and the savage onslaught of fire and earthquake, they more adequately served their functions and assumed their ultimate proportions. The walls of these buildings were, on the whole, constructed of adobe bricks, although certain portions were occasionally built of stone. Rock foundations mortared with adobe mud were the general rule. Structural stability of walls was gained simply by mass thickness, and comparatively low ceiling height.

This was the type of architecture the affluent Spanish dons used for their hospitable and commodious homes, which they glorified with a transplanting of the warmth and color of their ancestral lands.

Although the essence of adobe architectural design in Santa Barbara was not so much a perpetuation of an historic style as the logical expression of a particular type of building material, it possessed certain characteristics that it had acquired from historic sources.

From old Spain there emanated an architectural influence which, in itself, was composed of many overlapping trends from most of the countries of Europe, and even from the Orient. Although Spain borrowed profusely, she managed to infuse a warmth into the architecture of Andalusia. This is especially true of the farmhouses of Southern Spain.

It is this influence, greatly simplified, which has made itself felt largely in the adobe houses built in California shortly after the missions were established. The directness and honesty of this adobe architecture has kept it free from the over-elaborate design that was prevalent in Mexico. Then, too, the fact that the California Indians were not skilled in the art of building and possessed no architectural background, made adobe building much more primitive than it was in Mexico, where the native Indian traditions in building, and their skills in arts and crafts, assisted in developing a more elaborate expression.

In California, the first buildings were constructed after the manner of Indian sun-baked, soil houses; but soon there developed structures of architectural import.

Shortly after 1800, American travelers and settlers from the Atlantic coast came and brought with them definite ideas of construction which they incorporated in their new adobe homes.

A few of Santa Barbara's old adobes, built under these combined influences of Indian, Spanish, Mexican, and Eastern-Colonial architecture, are described in the following pages. All are interesting relics of a romantic bygone age, while several still lend themselves to their original purpose as charming, livable dwellings.

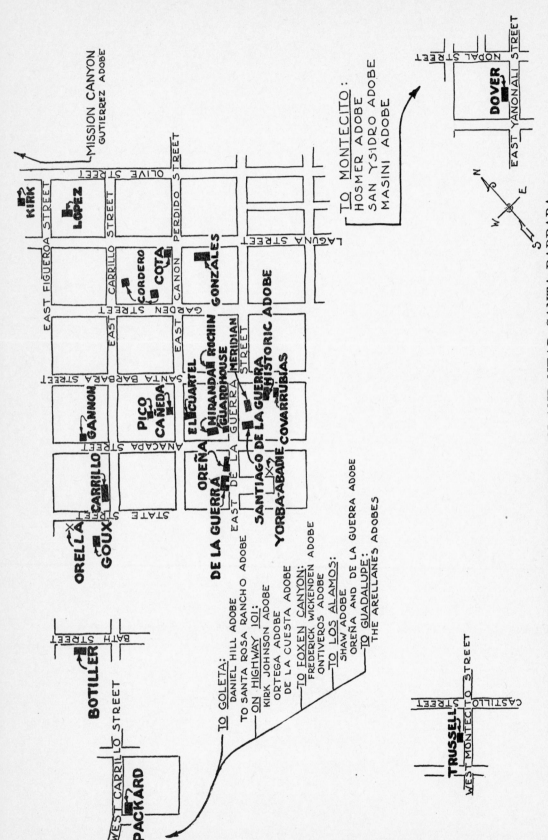

MAP SHOWING OLD ADOBES IN AND NEAR SANTA BARBARA

EL CUARTEL

El Cuartel, the oldest adobe in Santa Barbara, was once a part of the Spanish Presidio barracks. In its restored condition it serves as offices for the Mission Council of the Boy Scouts of America.

EL CUARTEL

EL CUARTEL IN 1885

EL CUARTEL—SANTA BARBARA'S OLDEST ADOBE

About the time that the American Revolution on our eastern seaboard was drawing to a close, the first adobe house in Santa Barbara, and one of the few of that period extant in California, was built as a part of the southwest side of the quadrangle of Santa Barbara's Spanish presidio. The Santa Barbara Mission was not begun until four years later.

It may seem a far cry to that little known period when the early pioneers of Latin blood erected their missions and their bastions on the Pacific slope. Yet there has always been something impressive about the memories that cling to the adobe houses of the early dons and the padres from Spain. The atmosphere of those bygone days is more to be cherished than subsequent recollections of a war, a century ago, when the justice of the Yankee cause was not unmixed with Anglo-Saxon concern for the development of vast and fertile lands, and perhaps of gold.

Today, young America is served within the hoary walls of El Cuartel (the barracks of the old Spanish presidio); for it is here that the Mission Council of the Boy Scouts of America formulates plans for the guidance, activities, and well-being of the boys who are enrolled in the cub packs and scout troops that fall within its jurisdiction. This historic setting, rich in local lore, may well stir the imagination of modern boys. Such a prized heirloom brings to mind a colorful and romantic past in which the zealous friars and soldiers of Spain played their part along with the gaily-caparisoned **rancheros** in the carefree life of those first California settlers. It was a golden age in which the people worked and played, danced and sang in enjoyment of the simple, natural pleasures.

As a part of the original Presidio Real, established in 1782 by order of Governor Felipe de Neve, and in the presence of Captain Jose Francisco Ortega and the renowned Padre Presidente, Fray Junipero Serra, this historic house conjures up memories that continue to fire the hearts of Californians.

Captain Ortega, the commander of the Catalan "leather-jackets" who had marched with Serra to San Diego in the spring of 1769, although not receiving the appointment as Governor of California, as the worthy padre had urgently requested, was, nevertheless, selected by Governor Felipe de Neve as the first **comandante** of Santa Barbara's presidio. It was under Captain Ortega's supervision that El Cuartel was planned and built.

Don Raimundo Carrillo, who succeeded Ortega as **comandante,** was next to have charge of El Cuartel. Don Raimundo, whom the Padre Presidente had united in marriage to Tomasa Lugo, some years before, was the founder of the illustrious Carrillo family in California. The popular moving picture star, Leo Carrillo, is the modern scion of this family. The don had several sons but only one daughter. The latter, Maria Carrillo, married a young Spanish lieutenant of the presidio, Jose Antonio de la Guerra. Together they founded another of California's first families. Lieutenant de la Guerra succeeded his father-in-law, becoming the third and most revered, **comandante** of the Santa Barbara Presidio. His long and notable stewardship of El Cuartel and the presidio affairs, together with his personal qualities and the grace and charm of his lovely wife endeared the de la Guerra family to all who knew them.

The old presidio house has played its part under the flags of Spain and Mexico, and now, under the Stars and Stripes it silently bears testimony that the craftsmen of those olden times did their work well. At first it was a portion of a group of one-story houses used for soldiers' quarters. Being at the end of the row and at the entrance, it was used for the guard. In the 1840's Jose Jesus Valenzuela lived there and was assigned the duty of checking the soldiers in and out of the presidio. Valenzuela continued to occupy the place even after the days of the presidio, being employed as a messenger-postman to carry letters and important papers from Santa Barbara to the large **ranchos** that surrounded the town. The house was deeded to him, through the good graces of Don Jose Antonio de la Guerra, while California was under Mexican rule.

The accompanying drawing shows El Cuartel, viewed from the west, as the Valenzuela house in the early eighties. The porch and front door, in those days, were on the side that now faces Santa Barbara's post office. A venerable pepper tree stands at a spot where the wooden well-head and windlass appear in the drawing. The water from this well was particularly **agua dulce** (sweet water), being so popular with the neighbors that the windlass was in almost constant motion. At the time of the picture the windows were of the double-hung type. By their division into six panes and their louvred shutters, they show a Yankee influence that swept the place in the early fifties, having come around Cape Horn with New England settlers.

The historic El Cuartel adobe still retains, even in its much remodeled state, a forthright attribute of simple structural honesty, which is one of the commendable qualities of most of the old adobe houses. Its low, thick walls bespeak stability and permanence; the red-tile roof adds a warmth to contrast with the plain whitewashed walls and the verdure round about.

These walls are two feet thick and made of adobe bricks laid in adobe mortar, plastered with more adobe, and then whitewashed. The original hand-made tile of the roof has been replaced by machine-made tile which is laid over shingles. The building consists of two rooms. The largest is fourteen by twenty-four feet and has a high ceiling with sturdy timber roof trusses. A fireplace is located adjacent to the entrance, and in the opposite wall a bookcase is built deep into the adobe. On the part that was originally the rear yard, there has been created a patio thirty feet wide, running the length of the two original rooms. Here trees and shrubs, a small pool, and a seat cut into the adobe wall create an atmosphere of quaint charm. Part of the north wall was removed when Canon Perdido Street was improved, as the structure was built at a slight angle to that street and one corner encroached on the sidewalk space.

It may be of interest to relate the derivation of the name of this street, Canon Perdido (Lost Cannon), on which the historic adobe faces. It was early in the spring of 1848 that the American brig "Elizabeth" was wrecked on the coast near Santa Barbara. A gun from the ship remained buried in the sand, but the American officer in command of the port got the idea that the cannon had been stolen and an incident was precipitated. The affair was finally adjusted by Don Pablo de la Guerra, after the citizens of Santa Barbara had been taxed $500 on account of the disappearence of the weapon. A cannon reputed to be this one was later found and now reposes in the tower-museum of Santa Barbara's courthouse.

THE CANEDA ADOBE

This drawing shows a restoration
on paper as the building may have
appeared in the 1880's. In the fall
of 1944 the frame building that
concealed the Caneda adobe was
razed and the old house emerged
in full view from East Canon Perdido Street. Mr. and Mrs. Elmer
H. Whitaker have restored and enlarged the old structure but retained the lines and the spirit of
the place. This is the second oldest adobe house in Santa Barbara.

THE CANEDA ADOBE

THE CANEDA ADOBE

This historic adobe, for many years concealed behind a mid-Victorian frame house at 121 Canon Perdido Street, was built in 1782 shortly after the Valenzuela adobe, the previously mentioned El Cuartel. Its outside wall formed a part of the original presidio enclosure, the building itself having been built on the inside of the northwest wall of the presidio quadrangle and near its westerly corner. This house did not stand alone. There was a solid row of adobes adjoining each other to the northeast until they reached the presidio church. There was another adobe house in the same row of houses and a few yards to the southwest. This was originally the westerly corner of the presidio. Across the street stands El Cuartel. Contiguous with the Caneda house on the northeast stood the Maldonado adobe. It was here that in the sixties and seventies Jose Maria Maldonado wrapped cigarettes by hand and delivered them to local hotels and liquor dispensaries.

When California was under Mexican rule, the Caneda house was granted to Jose Maria Caneda, a presidio soldier, and subsequently became the home of Narciso Caneda, who later fought in the war between the States. He was a well known Santa Barbara musician, recognized as a cornetist.

The accompanying sketch shows the house as it may have appeared in the early eighties. Its outlines have been accurately drawn from the original structure, with the setting restored from the recollections of Frank L. Birabent and of Steven Valenzuela, who in the 1880's lived in the adobe house across the street.

In 1876 it was deeded to A. A. Oglesby by J. E. Goux and Pedro Baron. On November 5, 1878 it was acquired from A. A. Oglesby by Pedro Baron. Baron was a native of France who had become a prominent Barbarino. In 1865 he married Altagracia Leyva of Santa Barbara. Although the Barons first lived on Las Cruces Rancho and later at La Quemada, the old Caneda adobe was often used by them when they came to town; but it being too small for the Barons and their six children, Pedro, about 1880, contracted with Colonel Fernandes, a veteran of the Union forces, to build the two-story frame house which until 1945 obscured the old adobe. It is of interest to note that Fernandes made it a habit to wear his carpenter's apron on all occasions whether it was a wedding, a funeral, or merely a fiesta.

It was in this frame house and in the adobe behind it that the Baron family lived for about twenty years. At the turn of the century the property was sold for $2,500, with a $25 down payment, to Albert W. Weekly, who made his home there for about twenty years. Weekly, in his youth, drove the horse-car that operated from Main and Spring Streets to Agriculture Park in Los Angeles.   On his arrival in Santa Barbara he married Rebecca Tarr, daughter of one of the first English mariners to settle in the Channel City.   Rebecca's mother was a native of Santa Barbara.   During the Weekly occupancy of the old adobe it was kept well.   About it and the frame house in front there grew a garden of quaint charm.   Old-fashioned stock, gilly-flowers, hollyhocks and roses gave their color and fragrance.   In those days Albert Weekly drove a horse-drawn hack for the Santa Barbara Transfer Company.   When motor cars became more common, he acquired a commercial automobile to assist him in conducting a produce business dealing principally with fruit and melons.   In the winter months he developed a discriminating clientele for the homemade tamales for which Mrs. Weekly fast became famous.   In 1920 the property was sold to Elmer H. Whitaker of Montecito.

As was the fashion in the adobe days, a porch fronted the entire building.   Door and window reveals are shown on the inside, and four-panel doors and double-hung windows muntined into six panes to each sash are reminiscent of the Yankee influence and were probably added to the original structure in the 1850's.

Although this house was not a conspicuous example of adobe building, it possesses, in its restored and enlarged condition, a simple charm conforming to the best in Santa Barbara's old adobe domestic architecture.

CASA ARRELLANES

At 800 Santa Barbara Street on the corner of De la Guerra Street formerly stood the Arrellanes adobe house. This was probably the first house of consequence built in Santa Barbara outside of the confines of the presidio. It was begun by a Spaniard in 1795 and for many years was used as a residence combined with a general store where merchandise and liquors were sold. Several additions were made by subsequent owners before it became the home of Don Teodoro Arrellanes, a large, fine-looking **ranchero**, and his wife, Dona Josefa Rodriguez Arrellanes. Don Teodoro was the grantee of several neighboring **ranchos.** Their three children were raised here and still another generation of the Arrellanes family occupied it.

On Mach 5, 1910, it was sold to the Neighborhood House Association and was almost immediately remodeled. This is one of the first restorations in Santa Barbara of an historic old house converted to public use. It was during this remodeling that the original columns of the Arrellanes adobe were replaced by the elaborately carved and fluted ones that had formerly graced the corridors of the patio and the **portales** of the palatial Aguirre house. These columns were unearthed by Charles Edwards from a pile of old lumber, roofing tile and debris at the rear of the property once occupied by the Aguirre home, which stood a few yards east of the present Casa Carrillo. Roof tile from the same pile of discarded material was salvaged and re-used on the Arrellanes adobe restoration.

In the earthquake of 1925 the old Neighborhood House of adobe was badly damaged; as a result it was taken down and the present stucco house built in its place. The central portion of this building is reminiscent of the old adobe, although it is about fifty feet northeast of the original site. In the new building, two wings were added. The open porch columns were taken from the Neighborhood House, which had acquired them when remodeled in 1910, and were incorporated in the present stucco structure. A column of the entrance porch to the north wing differs from the columns on the main porch of the central portion and probably was one of the front **portales** columns of the old Aguirre adobe. The design and detail of both types of columns are of especial interest, as they are a unique example of carved columns. About two and one-half feet of the original columns have been sawed off at the bottom to make them fit their present position on the Neighborhood House. They are shown on page 87.

THE COVARRUBIAS ADOBE

The sketch shows the appearance of the Covarrubias house in 1923. It was subsequently restored and is used as headquarters by Rancheros Visitadores, an equestrian organization that perpetuates the atmosphere of early California.

THE COVARRUBIAS ADOBE

CASA COVARRUBIAS

The adobe homestead of the Covarrubias family, located at 715 Santa Barbara Street, about ten feet south of the present location of the "Historic Adobe," was built in 1817 by Don Domingo Carrillo, the son of Jose Raimundo Carrillo, who is regarded as the founder of the Carrillo family in California. Don Domingo built it for his bride Concepcion Pico, the sister of Governor Pio Pico and General Andres Pico. In 1853 this was the property of Joaquin Carrillo and soon after was acquired by Don Jose Maria Covarrubias, a native of France and naturalized citizen of Mexico. When Don Jose married Maria Carrillo, the daughter of Don Domingo, the house became the home of the Covarrubias family for the next fifty years. Don Jose, who in his youth was a school teacher, was the first federal elector from California. When he delivered California's electoral vote of 1852 for Franklin Pierce he was welcomed at the wharf by the entire Tammany Hall. His son, Don Nicolas Andres Covarrubias, who was for many years the sheriff of Santa Barbara County and United States marshall, and was noted for his fine horsemanship, also lived here. This same house was once occupied by Don Pio Pico. It was then that the last meeting of the assembly of congress in California under Mexican rule was held within its walls.

It is built in the shape of a letter L and contains four high, spacious rooms that are lighted from both sides. The main room or **sala** is fifty-five feet long and retains its original adobe-wall construction, although buttresses have been added on the outside as a precaution against seismic disturbances. A scrutiny of the original construction leads to the supposition that the house, which was built in the Mission period, was actually constructed by the Indians who built the mission buildings. It was originally roofed with mission tile supported on willow canes. Over the canes a layer of mud was placed and the tiles set in it. The age and historic associations of the Covarrubias house make it one of the most venerable adobes in Santa Barbara.

CASA DON JOSE ANTONIO JULIAN DE LA
GUERRA Y NORIEGA

This plan shows the original home,
and its restoration as executed by
James Osborne Craig and architect
Carleton Winslow in 1919. Re-
drawn from Historic American
Building Survey material.

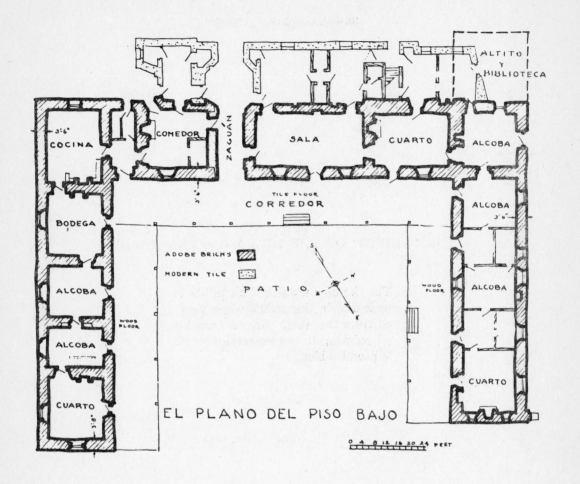

PLAN OF THE DE LA GUERRA ADOBE

THE "ALTITO" OF THE DE LA GUERRA ADOBE

The sketch shows the "altito" as it
appeared in the 1880's when viewed from the west. Drawn from an
oil painting in the possession of T.
Wilson Dibblee.

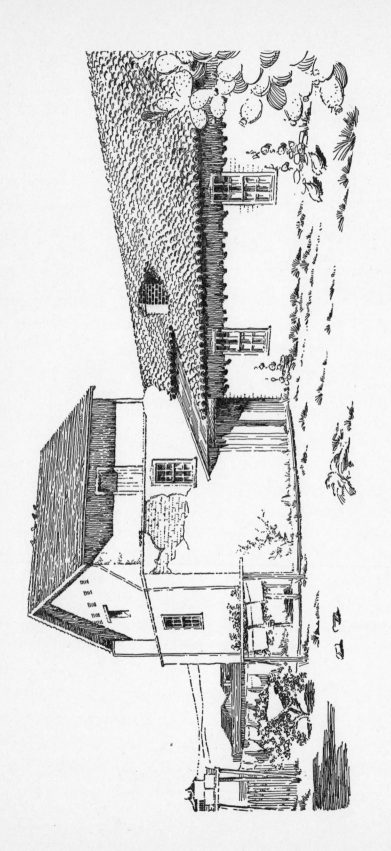

THE "ALTITO" OF THE DE LA GUERRA ADOBE

DE LA GUERRA ADOBE IN 1890

CASA DE LA GUERRA

About thirty-five years after the founding of the Presidio Real of Santa Barbara, the de la Guerra home was begun. Don Jose Antonio Julian de la Guerra y Noriega is, as is indicated by the double surname, descended from the de la Guerra line on his paternal side and maternally from the Noriega family. As both are said to be of noble tradition, Don Jose was indeed a "blue blood." He first came to Santa Barbara as a lieutenant stationed at the presidio. Through his marriage to Dona Maria, the only daughter of the presidio's **comandante**, Raimundo Carrillo, he founded in California one of the oldest and most prominent families of the state.

The de la Guerra home was the scene of many social, military, and political gatherings that have played a part in the early history of Santa Barbara. It still holds the memory of this beloved **comandante** and his kindly, charming wife, who won the esteem of all who knew her.

The de la Guerra adobe home, the foremost of the houses of Santa Barbara, was begun in about 1819 but was not completed until 1826. Many of its roof timbers and door and window lintels are of local sycamore; others may have been brought in by sailing vessels. The floor plan was built around three sides of an ample patio. Here, Richard Henry Dana related in "Two Years Before the Mast," affairs of state and events of social gaiety took place. In the 1890's, the walls were covered with clapboards. As a matter of protection against the weather, many adobes were treated in this manner. In 1919, the original porches were widened and the posts replaced and the roofs covered with tile. The simplicity and genuine earthy quality of this early structure has been retained by its modern restorers. The late James Osborne Craig and Carleton M. Winslow, architect, were the builders responsible for the restoration.

The house stands several steps above the patio. The porch roofs, which were once carried on square brick piers, and later by built-up, wooden columns, are now supported by solid, wooden posts.

A part of the building that faced the rear yard has been razed. This was the "altito", a three-story tower-like element. Although space in this article will not be utilized to go further into the fascinating history or detailed description of an historic landmark that is so well known and loved by all Santa Barbarans, there may still be those who have not heard of the "altito." The "altito" stood at the southeast corner of the present inner patio, a few yards from the present El Paseo and "Street in Spain". It was here that Don Jose Antonio kept his library on the second floor and his money and accounts on the third floor. There are stories told about his sons who, on occasions, augmented their allowances by coins from his money chest, obtaining them by the use of a bamboo pole inserted through a crack by the door. The pole was equipped on its far end, with a pad covered with tar. The coins adhered readily to the sticky substance while being withdrawn from the chest and through the crack.

The Casa de la Guerra was sold in 1945 to Mr. and Mrs. Fred Trevillian.

THE PEDRO MASINI ADOBE HOUSE

This fine old example of the cantilevered balcony type of house is reputed to have been built in 1820.
There are few two-story adobes in
the Santa Barbara area. The over-
hanging balcony suggests houses
that were more common in the environs of Monterey, California.

THE PEDRO MASINI ADOBE HOUSE

THE MASINI ADOBE

At the foot of Ortega Hill, now 29 Sheffield Drive in Montecito, stands the Pedro Masini adobe house. It was located on an
old stage road from Los Angeles to Santa Barbara, in the sixties
the principal artery of overland traffic. It was a regular stage
stop. This structure is the oldest two-story adobe house still standing in the Santa Barbara area. Masini did not build it, if its reputed date of construction, 1820, is correct, but purchased the
property in 1869 from N. Couts.

Subsequent to his occupancy, an Italian, G. B. Trabucco, lived
there alone and tended the vineyards that surrounded it. As his
expenses were small and the earnings large, he amassed a considerable sum of money. One day in December of the year 1881,
Trabucco went to town and on the way home stopped at a tavern
to have refreshments with some acquaintances who, it has been
stated, learned of his hoarded money. That night, the recluse had
callers at the old adobe house. He served them wine, as was evident by the jug and four glasses that were found a few days later
when Trabucco's mutilated body was discovered in the kitchen of
his house. There was ample evidence that he had been brutally
tortured in an effort to find the hiding place of his money. Two
canvas shot-bags, believed to have been filled with coin, were found
on the floor. It is presumed that they were hidden in a sack of
barley. This crime is one of the few murders that have stirred
Santa Barbara.

A few years later the Masini house was purchased by Josefa
Etchas and became the home of her brother's family, Juan Arroqui
and his wife, Bernarda Bertha Lopez Arroqui. Their daughter,
Mrs. Helena Meyer, recalls that her grandfather, Marino Palomares
y Lopez, who came to Santa Barbara as a boy in 1815, stated that
the adobe was built when he was a youth. Lopez died more than
forty years ago at the age of eighty-five.

In spite of the vicissitudes that this old adobe has passed
through, there has been little change in its outward appearance.
The interior has been modernized in many respects. The kitchen,
even in the time of Trabucco's tenancy, was in the one-story part.
The fire was built on a hearth in one corner and without a chimney.
The rafters, walls and beams became heavily incrusted with a
black deposit. Originally there was but one large room below in
the two-story element and one above. Although it suffered but
little damage in the earthquake of 1925, new beams were added

to strengthen the ceilings.

This house, which has been recorded in measured drawings by the Historical American Building Survey, is one of the more perfect examples of the cantilevered balcony type of Monterey architecture in Southern California.

THE YORBA-ABADIE ADOBE

In 1925, before the earthquake of
that year, the Yorba-Abadie adobe
appeared as shown here. The house
no longer stands, but the bricks
from its walls have been incorporated in the Caneda adobe as restored.

THE YORBA-ABADIE ADOBE

A FRAGMENT OF THE SALA WAINSCOT
(YORBA-ABADIE ADOBE)

THE YORBA-ABADIE ADOBE

This adobe house was situated just south of the Santa Barbara
City Hall and facing the De la Guerra Plaza. It was built before
1826 by Joaquin Maitorena, a lieutenant in the Spanish army. It
was here that he brought his bride, Ysabel Yorba. Ysabel Yorba
was a descendant of Antonio Yorba, who in 1769 was one of Pedro
Fages' original Catalan volunteers and in 1777 was corporal of the
San Francisco Company. Her mother was Josefa Grijalva Yorba.
Maitorena died in Mexico in 1830, leaving Senora Maitorena without children. The widow Maitorena adopted a young woman, Isabel
Lugo and her daughter Refugio. Senora Maitorena preferred to
be called Ysabel Yorba. In 1863 Refugio married Dominique
Abadie, a native of France, who had come to California in 1849 and
settled in the Channel City in 1850 to open a mercantile business.
There were three children born of this marriage, Felicidad, Juan,
and Domingo. In 1868 Abadie was murdered in a quarrel. The
beautiful Felicidad married the well-known American artist, Alexander Harmer, who made his home in Santa Barbara in 1893 and
devoted his palette to painting California scenes. This house was
his home for more than a quarter of a century. He died in January,
1925. Although it was not one of the largest of the old Spanish
houses in Santa Barbara, it was one of the most attractive on its
exterior. Its interior was elaborately decorated. There was nothing
primitive about its detail or decoration. A decorator from Europe,
whose name has been lost but who was popularly called El Pintor,
was responsible for most of the excellent interior treatment. The
three large rooms of the western portion opening onto the front
veranda were plastered with adobe mud and covered with wallpaper. The **sala,** the center room of these three, had a heavy
molded cornice and chair rail, both lavishly painted in colors. The
wallpaper in this room was hand-painted. From the chair rail to
the floor a wainscot was painted directly on the adobe plaster. This
wainscot is of unusual importance and is shown in the accompanying drawing. The design and decorative treatment of this
wainscot follows closely the classic precedent, which at the time of
its painting, about 1850, was especially popular with discriminating decorators the world over, who were stimulated by the architectural discoveries widely publicized as a result of excavations
at the ancient city of Pompeii. El Pintor, who executed these designs in the Yorba-Abadie adobe, was evidently inspired by this
Pompeian source. The background of the **sala** dado was a deep red-

brown with white floral festoons draped upon it. In the room north of the **sala** the dado was painted in imitation of marble, realistically executed with black markings. The double-hung windows were provided with shutters to open in against the deep reveals. A pair of these shutters, still preserved, are solid and in two panels with raised moulds framing the panels. Each panel is decorated in its center with a design combining birds and flowers painted on a deep buff background. The corners of the panels have conventional designs. The fineness of detail was not confined to the interior painting but was carried out on the exterior as well. One instance may be observed in the delicately tapered spindles of the front porch balustrade. These refinements of millwork were added to the house some years after its original construction. The two pairs of double doors, one opening into the **sala** from the street on the west and the other from the patio on the east, recall an incident told by a son of Alexander Harmer, who recounts that when he was a youngster, a mounted officer of the law caught him with his playfellows raiding a carrot patch back of the old city hall and gave chase. These massive house doors being ajar, the culprits darted in and the rider followed in hot pursuit, riding through the doorway into the **sala** and through it into the patio. The front veranda in later years was trimmed with a wainscot of Pompeian red and a soft cream-colored wall above it. Such painted wainscots have long been popular in Mexico and Spain, as they serve the double purpose of keeping the light-colored walls from showing wear and grime and at the same time temper the rays of the sun which reflect too brightly from a white surface.

This historic adobe suffered serious structural damage during the earthquake of 1925, and after that the western part was unoccupied. The front wall, which leaned slightly, was propped up for a time, but in October 1938 the veranda and this wall were pulled down and the house was reduced to a shambles. In June, 1942, steps were taken to protect the remainder by placing a cement cap and shingle roof over the unprotected walls.

The house has now been taken down brick by brick and incorporated in the reconstructed Caneda adobe.

THE RAFAEL GONZALES ADOBE

The Gonzales adobe, after restoration by A. L. Murphy Vhay, is a striking example of old Spanish architecture remodeled and restored for modern living.

THE RAFAEL GONZALES ADOBE

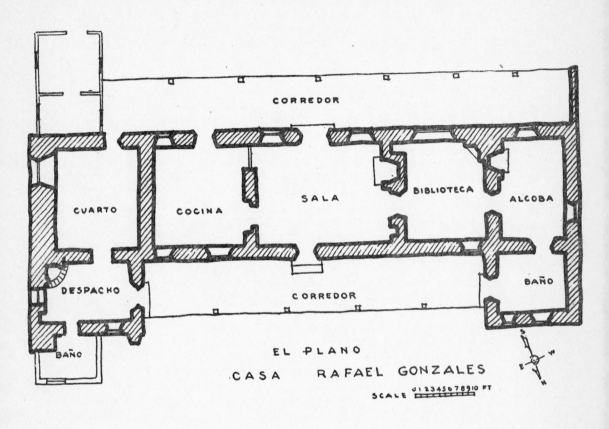

CORREDOR

CUARTO   COCINA   SALA   BIBLIOTECA   ALCOBA

DESPACHO   CORREDOR   BAÑO

BAÑO

EL PLANO

CASA   RAFAEL GONZALES

SCALE 0 1 2 3 4 5 6 7 8 9 10 FT

CASA RAFAEL GONZALES FLOOR PLAN

THE RAFAEL GONZALES ADOBE

Adobe architecture in Santa Barbara is more native than its native sons. It dates back to the time of the Spanish dons and is a priceless characteristic of former days. Thoroughbred adobe houses have not the slightest resemblance to the mongrel creations of wood and stucco that, all too often, clutter the California countryside and are incorrectly called "Spanish houses".

The adobe house popularly called the Casa de Ramirez, located at 835 Laguna Street in Santa Barbara, is a fine example of the California house of the Spanish period, having been erected about 1825 by Rafael Gonzales, a descendant of the family to which the King of Spain had granted large acreage. Gonzales married an Italian girl and brought her to this house as their home. Don Rafael was **alcalde** of Santa Barbara in 1829. One of his daughters, Salome Francisca Ventura Gonzales, married Cristobal A. Ramirez on April 26, 1865, and the old homestead was deeded to her on March 17, 1866, and became known as the Ramirez adobe. Senora Ventura Gonzales de Ramirez lived in this house until a few months before her death in 1923, when it was sold to A. L. Murphy Vhay.

The stonework at the base of some of the exterior walls was added as a matter of protecting the adobe from erosion where it was most exposed to the splash of eaves-drip. The main walls are of adobe bricks about 10 inches by 21 inches by 4 inches and laid in ¾ inch adobe-mortar joints. The exterior is covered by a lime whitewash. The walls of the porches, however, have been plastered. The structural woodwork on the under side of the porch roof is whitewashed to match the walls. The brick fireplaces and chimneys were added at the time of restoration, the exposed brick having been given a thin coat of whitewash. The door and window openings are spanned by timber lintels about three inches thick. The roof tile were hand-made by the Indians in the heyday of the mission. They are about twenty-four inches in length and eleven inches wide, laid at random. Their color varies. The exterior walls are a pale cream, with trim and sash and doors a blue-green. Some doors are whitewashed.

There have been some changes, some improvements, although the original plan, a long rectangle formed of twenty-four inch adobe walls on three sides and a four-foot wall on the southeast, from which direction the severe rains come, has remained unchanged. At first the floors were of packed earth, then of wood; at present they are of square hand-made tile. Above the rafters is a sheathing of saplings, which serves as a ceiling. Several windows have been added to the southwest side, which was originally the front. The garden and patio are fine replicas of such features in the California-Spanish period.

The Gonzales adobe is one of the best examples of the manner in which modern Americans have acquired and restored the old Spanish homes.

THE EMIL GOUX ADOBE

Part of this house may have
been built as early as 1812.
Although it stands surrounded by business buildings, it
retains its character of early
Santa Barbara.

THE EMIL GOUX ADOBE

THE GOUX ADOBE

This sun-baked adobe-brick house, situated in the rear of 1015 State Street, is in the heart of Santa Barbara's business district and is surrounded by commercial buildings so that it is completely hidden from the street. When access is finally gained to its small plot planted with trees, shrubs and vines, it is evident that the old adobe has overcome its modern environment and continues to exhale a breath of olden times. The house was built in the fore part of the nineteenth century, perhaps as early as 1812. Verifying this date of construction is the evidence discovered through the earthquake of 1925, when plaster peeled from the walls, revealing that the old adobe had passed through a previous seismic disturbance of major proportions that had opened cracks in the walls which had been filled and patched on that previous occasion. This is presumed to have been the earthquake of 1815.

The property belonged to Maria Antonio Feliz in 1853. Soon after that it was acquired by Jules Emil Goux, a native of Lyons, France, who came to Santa Barbara and became the bookkeeper for Abadie's general merchandise store, which was located at a spot in front of the present Lobero Theatre. In the 1860's Goux and a partner, Levy, opened a general merchandise store of their own and later engaged in the liquor business. From a perusal of the old records of Santa Barbara County it is evident that Emil Goux was a principal party in many important land transactions. His wife was Maria Caneda, a native of Santa Barbara. Emil Goux had five sons, Juan, Tomas, Augustine, Anastacio and Emilio and a daughter, Anna Goux Cota. Tomas and Augustine conducted a liquor store at the corner of State and Figueroa Streets. Tomas Goux, who married a daughter of John Longway, made his home in the Goux adobe. He and his wife, who were without children, both died there. The house passed to the possession of Attorney Julian Goux, who is the son of Augustine Goux.

On Goux's arrival in Santa Barbara he was the French consular representative there. It will be recalled that at that time Santa Barbara was a more important coastal port than Los Angeles. The young Frenchman, Goux, had several interesting schemes in mind. He brought silk worms and planted mulberry trees for them to feed upon and started the silk industry in Santa Barbara. It has been reported that the first American flag made of American manufactured silk was a result of this venture. Emil Goux, who was somewhat of an agriculturist, had plans to start a perfume factory, but that did not materialize. In the 1860's Goux was interested in a mercantile business in Santa Barbara, and thereafter engaged extensively in land transactions in Santa Barbara County.

The Goux house is built in the shape of an elongated rectangle with a porch across the front. There were originally three rooms, but one partition has been removed, leaving one large room towards the west and one small one on the east. In the southeast corner of the sala there is a fireplace with a wooden mantel. It is influenced by American Eastern-Colonial precedent. Frame additions have been added at the rear to give modern kitchen and bathroom facilities. The doorways and window openings are neatly trimmed with millwork. The north door of the easterly room has a head-casing and door, cut to conform to the ceiling slope.

The Goux house has the veneration achieved through extreme age. Its architectural lines and simple details have retained a distinctive flavor of halcyon days.

THE SANTIAGO DE LA GUERRA ADOBE

The Santiago de la Guerra adobe house, which still stands at 110 De la Guerra Street, is reputed to have been built as early as 1812. It has been extensively altered and restored. It it shown on a map of Santa Barbara as belonging, in 1853, to James Tryce. Santiago de la Guerra lived there at the time that Don Antonio Maria de la Guerra, his uncle, a former mayor of Santa Barbara and state senator, recruited eighty-four men for the volunter "Lancers," a cavalry company of native Santa Barbarans, eighty-three of whom spoke Spanish only. This company played a colorful part in the war between the States. Antonio became captain and Santiago first lieutenant. It was in the summer of 1864 that these volunteers walked from Santa Barbara to Drum Barracks at Wilmington, where they received their horses. They had got as far as Arizona when the war ended. The company was sent to San Francisco to be mustered out, returning to Santa Barbara by boat.

The old adobe house, which bears the name of Santiago de la Guerra, remained in the Tryce family for many years. In 1925, because of the earthquake, the north wall fell out. The house was purchased from Arturo Orena about 1930 and remodeled into studio apartments. It is so modernized that the exterior does not indicate the adobe construction.

THE CARRILLO ADOBE

This old adobe was restored by
Max Fleischmann and presented
to the Santa Barbara Foundation. It is perpetuated as an
historic landmark.

THE CARRILLO ADOBE

CULLIMORE

THE CARRILLO ADOBE

The Casa Carrillo is situated at 11 East Carrillo Street. It is a few yards southwest of the place where the beautiful Aguirre adobe once stood, and directly northeast of the adobe that was for many years occupied by the James Burke family and that also served at a later period as a storehouse for merchandise for the firm of Wilson, Park and Scott and eventually became the property of Captain Wilson.

This historic house was built about 1826 by Daniel Hill, born in Billerica, Massachusetts in 1799, who came to California in 1823 on the sailing vessel, "Rover". It was here that he brought his bride, Rafaela Luisa Ortega de Hill, a direct descendent of Jose Francisco Ortega, who came to San Diego in 1769 as commander of Spanish soldiers and in 1782 established the Presidio of Santa Barbara with Governor Felipe de Neve and Padre Junipero Serra. Hill, a sort of general factotum in Santa Barbara, had installed in this house the first wooden floor in the village of Santa Barbara. Here a daughter, Rosa Antonia Hill (who later married Nicholas A. Den) and five or six other children were born to Daniel Hill and Rafael Luisa Ortega de Hill. As Hill's home it housed the first American woman resident of Santa Barbara, Mrs. Thomas Oliver Larkin. She was then the young widow of Captain Holmes, who died at sea. She subsequently married Larkin. Her first child was Isabel, who was born in 1833 in this house and died there a year later. This was the first American child to be born in California. Lieutenant Raimundo Pacheco once occupied this house. He was killed in combat near Los Angeles while he was marching to the support of Governor Victoria. This was shortly after the birth of his son Don Ramualdo, who later became a governor of California under the American regime. He is the only governor of Spanish blood to have held that office subsequent to California's advent into the United States. Captain John D. Wilson married Ramona, the beautiful widow of Captain Ramualdo Pacheco, who lived in the old adobe with her two remarkable black-eyed sons by Pacheco and three daughters and one son by Wilson. At that time Dona Ramona Wilson's home was the most attractive rendezvous in Santa Barbara. All through the 1840's this house was in its glorious prime. In 1851 the Italian portrait painter, Barbieri, lived there. In 1852 a daguerreotypist opened a popular gallery on its front corridor.

In the 1860's it came into the possession of Guillermo and

Joaquin Carrillo, cousins and brothers-in-law. The Carrillo's were among the first Spanish families in California. The founder of that family on the Pacific slope was Don Raimundo Carrillo, who was married to Senorita Tomasa Lugo in 1769 by the Padre Presidente, Junipero Serra. Leo Carrillo, a cinema favorite, is the modern scion of this pioneer family.

Major Max C. Fleischmann acquired the property in recent years and gave it to the Santa Barbara Foundation to be preserved as a landmark.

CASA SAN YSIDRO

This old adobe, once the
home of the Olivera family,
now serves as an office suite
for the San Ysidro Ranch
Corporation.

CASA SAN YSIDRO

CASA SAN YSIDRO

Tomas Olivera, a son of Ignacio Olivera, who was a sergeant under the command of Captain Jose Francisco Ortega at the founding of the Presidio Real at Santa Barbara in 1782, was superintendent of those mission holdings on which the San Ysidro Rancho at Montecito is now located. It was in the early part of the century that the mission padres caused the adobe house, of which but one room still stands, to be built at San Ysidro. Its first occupant, Senor Olivera, had married the young widow of Jose del Carmen Osuna, of the San Diego branch of Osunas, and her daughter Eduarda came to live with her mother and step-father in the San Ysidro adobe. It was here that Senorita Eduarda first met her future husband, the young, high-tempered English mariner, William Benjamin Foxen, often called Julian Foxen, who later, upon the eve of his marriage, when he joined the Catholic Church, was baptized William Domingo Foxen. The grandchildren of the Foxen-Osuna union still relate the incidents of this meeting which have been told and retold for generations in the Foxen family.

The story goes that upon his first visit to the San Ysidro adobe the hardy Britisher looked about him for a light for his freshly-filled pipe. His use of the Spanish language was limited, but when his stern gray eyes caught the sparkle in the black ones of the lovely senorita, she divined his thoughts and produced the fire brand to ignite the young man's tobacco. The romance that ensued has given to Santa Barbara County many substantial citizens in whom a warmth of Latin culture has been fused with sterner English traits. The ancestry of the Osunas is quite another story, but in that connection it may be of interest to refer the reader to a book published by Lippincott in 1932 which recounts the vicissitudes of the Spanish duke who bore that name. It is entitled "The Perils and Fortune of the Duke of Osuna," and was written by Antonio Marichalar.

In 1868 the San Ysidro ranch property was acquired by a Maine Yankee, Bradbury T. Dinsmore, who planted the first orange grove of any size in the valley. An old stone house a few yards from the San Ysidro adobe holds the distinction of being the first citrus-fruit packing house in this section of California. When acquired by Dinsmore this place was a primitive wilderness. During his ownership it contained a plantation of a Chinese variety of dwarf bananas, and it was here that strawberry culture was first introduced into the valley. Supervisor Tom Dinsmore, whose father,

Augustus Dinsmore, inherited part of the place from his father, recalls that in the eighties the floors of the San Ysidro adobe were of asphalt from the Carpenteria asphalt seepage. This asphalt comes out of the hillside and hardens in the sun. It was used for making flat roofs and floors by mixing it with sand and boiling and spreading on hot. Later, the **rancho** belonged to Goodrich and Johnston. It was then that the yield of 300,000 oranges and 100,-000 lemons found a ready market. In 1935 the ranch passed into the hands of Alvin Carl Wingand and in 1936 to the ownership of the San Ysidro Ranch Corporation, of which Wingand is a principal stockholder. More than forty years ago the little old adobe was converted into an office on the San Ysidro estate, which, then and during the intervening years, has been a mecca for discriminating resort patrons. The property has maintained its high standard and has enhanced its reputation as a secluded fashionable hostelry.

Although this old adobe has gathered about it items of local lore and human interest, it possesses no outstanding architectural characteristics aside from its simple outline and quaint charm.

THE BENJAMIN FOXEN ADOBE

Redrawn from a sketch published in the Santa Barbara
News-Press of June 4, 1933.
The artist, whose name is not
known, drew the sketch from
a drawing made from mem-
ory by Mrs. Matilde Carteri,
daughter of Benjamin Foxen.

THE BENJAMIN FOXEN ADOBE

THE BENJAMIN FOXEN ADOBE IN FOXEN CANYON

About twelve miles from Santa Ynez Mission and twenty miles southeast of the town of Santa Maria lies Foxen Canyon, consisting of about 9,000 acres. This tract was granted as Rancho Tinaquaic to William Benjamin Foxen by the Mexican government in 1832. This is the same Foxen that was mentioned in connection with the San Ysidro adobe.

Foxen first appeared on this coast in 1820. He was born in Norwich, England in 1796. As a boy he sailed on merchant vessels and became first officer of a trader. He came around the Horn to California on the "Courier" and later engaged in the coastwise trade, plying between California and Mexico.

California appealed to Foxen. On a **rancho** near Santa Barbara he met Senorita Eduarda Osuna, reputed to be a descendant of the Count of Osuna of Spain. The young Englishman joined the Catholic Church, became a Mexican citizen, and married the lovely senorita. The Indians called him Don Julian, which, in Spanish, sounded something like William. He was thereafter known by this title. Foxen established a mercantile business in Santa Barbara, but after a few years he removed his family to the Mexican grant in Foxen Canyon. Here, about half way up the canyon, he built the Foxen adobe. Nothing but a mound of earth now remains to indicate the location of this house. Although grizzly bears infested the canyon, this sturdy pioneer developed a large stock ranch and erected a grist mill for Santa Ynez, La Purisima and neighboring **ranchos.**

When the Mexican War broke out, Foxen was in middle life and was a decidedly original and forceful character, respected and influential. Although a Mexican citizen, prudence and common sense prompted him to remain neutral.

He was large, powerful and fearless. Like many men of his time, he was rugged, outspoken, and at the same time noted for his truthfulness and the honor of his word. His booming voice, acquired doubtless in his sea-faring days, which in his later years seemed to vie with thunder, often caused recalcitrant Indians and turbulent citizens to cower. He was looked on as a sort of hero whose doings were often the cause of merriment when related by a good story-teller.

When in late December of 1846 Fremont and his half-starved American soldiers entered the upper end of his canyon and made camp on the spot now known as Fremont's Camp, the two men met and liked each other. Foxen allowed Fremont to kill some of his cattle and use his flour for much needed supplies. Santa Barbara's California Rancheros, organized their vaqueros to resist the Americans at Gaviota Pass. Foxen informed Fremont and with his young son, William Foxen, guided the Americans over the difficult San Marcos Pass to enter Santa Barbara without bloodshed.

Fremont's success seems to have been Don Julian's undoing. The Californians took revenge, pillaged the Foxen rancho, and perpetrated raid after raid until his ranch improvements became scarcely more than a shambles. Although ignored by California historians, it appears that Foxen contributed materially to California's capitulation to the Americans. Along with other hardships that were heaped upon this intrepid pioneer, came an accusation of murder in his later years, but his peers exonerated him on the plea of self-defense. In those days William Benjamin Foxen's firearms had of necessity become the only force potent to protect him and his interests.

Some uncomplimentary stories, perhaps caused by jealousy of the honor paid him as Fremont's guide, or simply the unfortunate habit of remembering the evil while interring the good with the bones, have been told about him. Those who knew him intimately gave him full credit for many admirable qualities which far outweighed his vices.

THE THOMAS HOSMER ADOBE

The original Hosmer adobe '
was probably flat-roofed, the
shingle covering having been
added later. The house as
shown in the sketch made
from an old photograph, was
later incorporated as the living room in the enlarged and
remodeled Hosmer home.

THE THOMAS HOSMER ADOBE

THE HOSMER ADOBE

The main room of this old adobe house, which was in the height of fashion in about 1835 and which became the home of Thomas Hosmer in 1871, still stands incorporated as a principal part of the present, more commodious, wood-frame house of Mrs. James Ord and Helen Hosmer of Montecito. It is located about one hundred yards southwest of the intersection of Valley Road and San Ysidro Road. A son of Maria Dominguez de Juarez, who owned the property in 1868, has stated that the old adobe was built in about 1830.

In 1871 Colonel Bradbury True Dinsmore, a Maine Yankee, who had come to Montecito in 1868 and acquired the San Ysidro Rancho on which he planted the first orange grove in the valley, purchased also the Juarez property including the old adobe. In the same year he deeded the latter to his daughter, Frances Dinsmore Hosmer, who had married another native of Maine, Thomas Hosmer. The bride had made the trip by steamer from Maine to the Isthmus of Panama and then up the Pacific to San Francisco, where the couple were married in 1863. In 1871 they came to Montecito Valley to establish their home in the two-room adobe that had been built years before by the Juarez family. Hosmer now engaged in raising almonds, plums and prunes and later planted an orchard of 700 orange trees. In the eighties Thomas Hosmer served for several years as supervisor of Santa Barbara County. Four children were born to the Hosmers and lived in the old adobe. They were William; Anne, who married Leslie Wrightson; Martha, who married James Ord; and Helen.

The Hosmer adobe in its original state was floored according to the prevailing Santa Barbara mode, which was accomplished by boiling asphalt seepage from the Carpenteria tar beds with sand and spreading it on a packed-earth base while still hot. The rooms were not ceiled, the exposed rafters being of rough-hewn timbers. The walls, which are three feet thick, afforded deep window seats, obviating the necessity of quite so many chairs, which were at that time hard to procure. At a somewhat later period the small window openings were fitted with double-hung, six-pane sash typical of American Eastern-Colonial precedent. It is of interest to note that the windows were small and few in number because of a tax which was imposed on the number and size of doors and windows. Still later the old roof was removed and replaced with a fashionable Yankee roof of shingles. At this time the rooms were ceiled

with cotton cloth tacked to the ceiling joists from beneath. Wood
floors now replaced the asphalt and the house became modern for
the 1870's. In 1925 the earthquake did it no structural damage but
caused some plaster to fall and made several minor cracks. These
were filled, and in the process of remodeling a corner fireplace was
added.

A few facts and some theories in regard to the ancestry of the
present occupants of this old adobe, by the name of Hosmer and
Ord, may well take their place as a part of the intriguing aura
which surrounds this heirloom from the days of Spain's occupancy
of California. The Hosmers trace their forebears to sturdy Colonial stock of our eastern seaboard. In fact, a musket used in the
American Revolution still hangs in the Hosmer adobe to bear evidence to the patriotism of an ancestor who fought with George
Washington. Even more remotely American is the almost legend-
ary claim voiced by the late Mrs. Thomas Hosmer that her people
have a blood relationship to a dusky Mohican princess.

THE BRUNO ORELLA ADOBE

At first possessing the characteristics of Spain and Mexico, this adobe later was clothed in a Victorian garb. The sketch shows its appear- in about 1890, drawn from a photograph in the possession of Mrs. Mercedes Carriaga. Only fragments of the house remain, incorporated in the restaurant, The Copper Coffee Pot.

THE BRUNO ORELLA ADOBE

THE BRUNO ORELLA ADOBE

The remaining portions of the Bruno Orella adobe house, located at 1029 State Street, have been incorporated in the modern restaurant, The Copper Coffee Pot. Previous to this occupancy the quaint old adobe interior had proved exceedingly attractive for the shops of the Paul Elder book store. This sturdy, thick-walled house was one of the landmarks of Santa Barbara. Only a part of the adobe walls and the patio outer wall still remain. The Copper Coffee Pot occupies a space equal to about the center third of the original house. Until a few years ago the hitching post that had held many a fractious steed stood in front of the house. It was finally demolished by an unruly automobile. This timber post was ornamented by a round top studded with nails so that the horses would not find it suitable material to chew on.

The records show that in 1859 the town of Santa Barbara deeded this property to Augustin Janssens; since then it has been in the possession of Maria Caneda, Juan Camorillo, E. J. Goux, William Abadie, Donat Cuirias and Charles E. Huse; in 1872 it became the home of Senor Bruno Orella and his wife Senora Mercedes Orella. The property now belongs to their daughter Mrs. Mercedes Carriaga. It is not definitely known when the original adobe was built, but Bruno Orella improved it and added many attractive architectural details. The house and yard were commodious and home-like. A cypress tree grew just north of it where business houses now stand. The accompanying drawing shows a tea-rose that climbed upon a porch column to display clusters of its blossoms from the housetop. A shrub (locturas), called "angels trumpet," with a trumpet-shaded blossom and rare fragrance, was the pride of the Orella garden. An adobe wall and lattice fence enclosed the premises.

The sala was large and the scene of frequent events of social gaiety. The house, although structurally of adobe and with a tile roof, was not a typically Spanish-California house when Bruno Orella's family lived there, for it had taken on the architectural dressings that were definitely Yankee. This is shown in the sketch which depicts porch columns and a balustrade of turned spindles.

THE AGUIRRE ADOBE

This palatial adobe has been
restored on paper as it may
have appeared in the 1850's.
It was drawn from an old
photograph and the recollections of pioneers. One of the
porch columns is used on the
restored Arrellanes house
(the Neighborhood House).

THE AGUIRRE ADOBE

COLUMNS FROM THE AGUIRRE ADOBE

The column with straight fluting is the only remaining example of the ones that graced the main **portales** facing the street. The inner patio was surrounded with columns with the twisted design. Several of these are in use on the porch of the Neighborhood House.

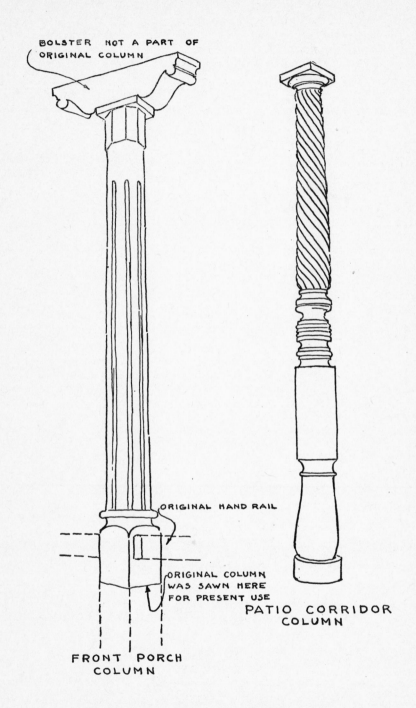

BOLSTER NOT A PART OF
ORIGINAL COLUMN

ORIGINAL HAND RAIL

ORIGINAL COLUMN
WAS SAWN HERE
FOR PRESENT USE

FRONT PORCH
COLUMN

PATIO CORRIDOR
COLUMN

COLUMNS OF THE AGUIRRE ADOBE

THE AGUIRRE ADOBE

The fine old Aguirre home fronted on what is now East Carrillo Street. It was built in the late thirties or early forties by Don Jose Antonio Aguirre, a wealthy merchant, shop owner, trader on the West Coast and extensive land owner. He was of French parentage but born in San Sebastian just over the border in Spain. A few yards west of the Aguirre adobe was the house of Captain John D. Wilson, who had married Ramona, the young and beautiful widow of Lieutenant Raimundo Pacheco, the father of a later governor of California, Romualdo Pacheco.

There are none left now who remember the famed beauty of the Aguirre adobe in its heyday. It has the reputation of having been a lovely exotic place. Don Jose surrounded himself with the elegance of an old-world civilization. Everything about the house bespoke hospitality, culture and abundance. It has been said that the daily appointments of his table were like those of a banquet. His first wife, Dona Francisca Estudillo Aguirrre, a member of the Estudillo family of San Diego, died in childbirth. Later he married her sister, Dona Rosario. Both were beautiful and refined women.

The house was built in the shape of a rectangle around four sides of a commodious patio. It was one-story but contained many rooms opening onto the patio corridors. Rock foundations elevated it a few feet above the prevailing grade. Its long street facade had a veranda in front of its entire length. Carved wooden columns supported the red tile roof. The sala was large and had a hardwood polished floor. It was palatially furnished. Sofas and chairs were of rosewood and mahogany, and rare paintings adorned the delicately frescoed walls. The patio was paved with stone and surrounded by open corridors with wood floors. Elaborately carved columns of a different design from those of the front supported this corridor roof. This was a favorite place for fiestas. It is said that Lobero, the early Santa Barbara impresario and musician at a later date held practice for his band in this patio. Still later, in April, 1847, Stevenson's regiment arrived in Santa Barbara and the officers were quartered in the Aguirre house. Postmaster Janssens conducted the affairs of Santa Barbara's federal post office from within its walls.

In 1880 the house was taken down, and the only vestiges of the Aguirre house that now remain are the elaborate columns which in 1910 were rescued from a pile of discarded material at the rear of the property where the Aquirre house once stood and were incorporated as columns on the porch of the Arrellanes house, which at that date was puchased and remodeled by the Neighborhood House Association. There were two types of these columns. One is seen in a single column on the porch of the north wing of the Neighborhood House and probably appeared originally on the front veranda of the Aguirre house. The other columns are now on the main veranda of the Neighborhood House. These originally graced the patio porch of the magnificent Aguirre mansion. The accompanying sketch shows these columns in detail.

MIRANDA ADOBE ENTRANCE

The Presidio Avenue entrance to the Miranda adobe was, in olden days, the main entrance, and the stable was near the Anacapa Street exposure, where a cocktail lounge is now located. Later the principal entrance faced Anacapa Street. The sketch shows the old doorway on the Presidio Avenue front. Today the Miranda house has been remodeled as a part of a modern restaurant.

MIRANDA ADOBE ENTRANCE

THE MIRANDA ADOBE

This solid adobe structure, faced with plaster and brightened by a coat of whitewash, was built about 1840. Every part of the building was necessarily simple. At the time of the American occupation it housed soldiers of the Mexican municipal garrison and later it was used by Miranda and his bride, Rita Layva, whom he married on February 20, 1851. The roof was formerly of hand-made, mission tile. The milled woodwork and trim was probably added in the early 1850's and shows the New England influence. Later it became the property of Teodoro Arrellanes and Pacifico Ortega, and eventually came into the possession of Jose Elazalde. In December, 1913, Francisco and Christina Nardi acquired possession of it. Today it stands extensively remodeled and enlarged to serve as a popular restaurant.

Miranda, the architect, was chosen to instruct Indians and supervise the building of a number of adobes in various parts of the town of Santa Barbara. The Miranda house is one of the old houses selected by the Historical American Building Survey to be recorded by measured drawings and photographs. These have been placed in the Archives in Washington.

SOLDIERS' QUARTERS AND GUARD HOUSE

Prior to 1846, the Guard
House and adjacent soldiers'
quarters, although not a part
of the old Spanish presidio,
quartered the Mexican garrison. F r e m o n t probably
caused the American flag to
be raised here when Santa
Barbara capitulated to the
Americans at the Christmas
season in 1846. The sketch
shows the place as it may
have appeared then. It is
now remodeled and enlarged.

SOLDIERS' QUARTERS AND GUARD HOUSE BEFORE
RESTORATION

THE GUARD HOUSE

A square adobe building at De la Guerra Street and Presidio Avenue was at one time used for an early Spanish-speaking school. Senora Calderon was its teacher. When Fremont entered Santa Barbara and took the village for the United States, Cipriana Llanos de Flores, the wife of the **comandante,** along with other "old-timers," has recalled that the American flag was raised on the pole in front of this house. Katherine Den Bell and Mrs. Ramona Trussell have stated that the first American flag was raised in front of the old St. Charles Hotel on State Street, which Fremont made his headquarters.

As the square building on De la Guerra Street was then used as a guard house adjacent to soldiers' quarters, it is quite possible that the American flag was raised in front of this municipal garrison guard-house as well as in front of Fremont's headquarters. A story has been passed down among the native Santa Barbarans of the beauty of that first showing of the **Bandera Nueva,** the Stars and Stripes. It is said that one senorita so strongly coveted it as material for a prospective skirt that she succeeded in getting possession of it after it was lowered in the evening; however, under threat of dire punishment, she was impelled to return it to its proper station before its absence became generally known.

The Guard House was originally on a slight knoll, but when De la Guerra Street was cut through and graded, the street level was about two feet below the former grade. This accounts for the height of the doorways and window openings, which were cut down at the bottom and had transoms inserted above. Old photographs of the structure show this adobe before the change was necessitated. The Miranda house, used as soldiers' quarters in the early forties, and the guard house adjacent to it were outside of the confines of the original Presidio Real of old Spanish days.

The Guard House is, in its remodeled state, incorporated in a building that also takes in the Miranda Adobe.

DE LA GUERRA AND ORENA ADOBE
AT LOS ALAMOS

The sketch shows the old
house as it appears after its
restoration by E d u a r d o
Orena Koch. It is as fine an
example of the old adobes as
any in California.

THE DE LA GUERRA AND ORENA ADOBE AT LOS ALAMOS

THE DE LA GUERRA AND ORENA ADOBE AT
LOS ALAMOS

This historic old adobe ranch house, located on the former routing of Highway 101, a few miles in a northerly direction from Los Alamos (the cottonwoods), must not be confused with the Santa Barbara house of Don Gaspar Orena or the homestead of Don Jose Antonio Julian de la Guerra y Noriega in Santa Barbara. Los Alamos de Santa Elena Rancho, on which the old adobe stands, was a part of the original Los Alamos Rancho, consisting of about 49,000 acres, granted to Jose Antonio de la Guerra y Carrillo on March 9, 1839, by Governor Juan Alvarado.

Don Jose Antonio was a son of Santa Barbara's venerated patriarch, Don Jose de la Guerra y Noriega. To the adobe, which the Indians of the near-by rancheria built for Don Jose Antonio on this grant, he brought his lovely bride, Dona Concepcion Ortega de la Guerra, who was noted far and wide for her beauty and who was a granddaughter of Captain Jose Francisco Ortega, who with Governor Felipe de Neve and the Padre Presidente Junipero Serra founded the Presidio of Santa Barbara. Subsequent to Don Jose Antonio's death and burial on a hillside near the old adobe, his brother-in-law, Don Gaspar Orena, bought the widow's property. Don Gaspar, whose full name was Gaspar Eugenio de Orena y Gomez de Escaudon, was born in Orena, a town of northern Spain, in 1824 in a province of that kingdom not far distant from the ancestral estates of his wife's forebears of the de la Guerra and Noriega strains. The Moors had never invaded this section, which is noted for the physical characteristics of the people, who possess unusual vigor and beauty. Don Gaspar, as a youth, studied medicine before coming to California in 1842. He married a daughter of the de la Guerra family, Dona Maria Antonia de la Guerra (widow of Cesareo Lataillade) who was born in the **comandante's** house at the Presidio Real at Santa Barbara. A daughter of this union, Mrs. Serena Orena de Koch, the widow of William Ignacio Koch, caused the restoration of the old Los Alamos adobe homestead, which she occupied during the summer months. Mrs. Koch was the mother of six children.

An air of hospitable gentility pervades its aging walls, combining with it an intangible aura of aristocracy, reminiscent of halcyon days when the grandees from old Spain enjoyed their pastoral California. This house is one of the most inspiring of the sun-dried earthen structures that date well back into the period when the flag of Mexico waved over the Pacific slope. Here the skeptical will be convinced that the fine art of gracious living has not vanished from the earth. The soft voice and sparkling eyes of the daughter of Don Gaspar turned back the hands of time when friends were shown into the ancient **sala**. Here one senses not only heirlooms of a hallowed past, but also an appropriate selection of furnishings that fit admirably into the pattern of life of those who now live there. As in the early days of California when its foremost citizens were of sea-faring stock, these modern world-traveling Americans are not hampered by national boundaries in the selection of furnishings nor fettered by man-prescribed vogues. A chest, a chair, and several valuable paintings have come from old Spain. From Mexico have come a lacquered table and a gorgeous lantern of hand-worked tin. A four-poster bed and a Federal desk long ago made their journey around Cape Horn from our Eastern Colonial coast to take their place in this **casa**. Here, too, a colorful **della Robbia** Madonna from Florence, Italy has been assigned to a secluded niche cut into the adobe wall; a tile plaque bears the de la Guerra coat-of-arms; and a portrait of Don Lorenzo de Orena, who fought for Spain against Napoleon, adds to the enchanting atmosphere of the place.

The floor plan of the house does not follow the symmetrical patterns that were prevalent in the town and ranch houses of its period, but seems to have been more perfectly fitted to its own particular hillside. The **sala** is the nucleus. The other rooms are inter-communicating and may also be reached by means of an open corridor. The plank floors and board ceiling supported by neatly-milled beams, beaded on the lower corners, are typical of the best work of their day. The walls and ceilings are painted white to simulate whitewash, and the floors have a natural aged warmth. Doors are four-paneled with raised moulds and window sash, six-paned. The interior trim of base and chair rail and casings is simply beaded on the edge and all painted white. On the exterior, the trim is olive green except on the loggia, where massive turned wooden spindles that bar a large window are painted a royal blue to match the color of fabrics of the porch furnishings. In the **sala** and the **comedor**, massive but simple gilded wood-carved candle chandeliers are a delight to the beholder and give the illusion of authenticity in every detail. Perhaps the most prized heirloom is an ancient crucifix brought from one of the ancestral homes in Spain. It stood for centuries over the entrance doorway there, and its worn and weatherbeaten appearance bears mute testimony to its extreme age, which has been estimated as more than four hundred years.

This historic old adobe, restored by Eduardo Orena Koch, continues to be admired above its more modern imitations. It is as fine an example of the spirit of adaptation of an old adobe house to modern enjoyment as may be found in all the length and breadth of California.

THE SAN CARLOS HOTEL

This historic structure built by Captain Alpheus Thompson no longer stands. But a replica in which to house an historical museum is contemplated.

THE SAN CARLOS HOTEL

THE SAN CARLOS HOTEL

This structure, built in 1834 by Captain Alpheus Thompson for his bride, Francisca Carrillo de Thompson, later became Colonel Fremont's headquarters when he took Santa Barbara for the Americans in December, 1846. It is stated that it was then that the first American flag was raised in Santa Barbara, on a pole in front of this adobe. In 1847 it was occupied by officers of Stevenson's regiment. Later it was converted into a hotel, being called the St. Charles or San Carlos Hotel. It was then a sort of family house with saloon and meat market on the first floor. No part of this building now stands.

Through the generosity of Mrs. John Russell Hastings and the cooperation of The Santa Barbara Historical Museum, it is planned to reproduce this structure in the orchard of the Captain Trussell house, which is owned by Mrs. Hastings. This reproduction is to be used as an historical museum.

THE FREDERICK WICKENDEN ADOBE

The ranch on which the Frederick Wickenden adobe stands was part of a Mexican grant bestowed upon Benjamin Foxen and was inherited from him by his daughter Ramona. About three miles below the spot in Foxen Canyon where Benjamin Foxen built his adobe home, which is now marked only by a mound of earth, stands the adobe home of Frederick Wickenden. Only the center portion is of adobe. This part was built by Frederick Wickenden with the help of Indians in 1862. Wickenden was a native of England, born in Portsmouth, November 18, 1825. At the age of twenty-five he went to Peru, where he superintended the construction of a railroad. He later journeyed up the west coast and finally settled in this place, where he engaged in raising sheep. In 1860 he married Ramona Foxen, the second daughter of Benjamin Foxen. Their nine children, six sons and three daughters, were raised here; all except three were born in this house. J. R. Wickenden, the present owner, is the youngest.

After Wickenden had built his house he added a storeroom on the west side and engaged in a general merchandise business. He also operated a post office for about forty years. This place was a stage stop between San Louis Obispo and Santa Barbara, so that the Wickenden place was a commercial and social center for the surrounding country for many years. In his later years Frederick Wickenden was known to his friends as "The Old Gentleman," a title which his gracious and kindly manners had earned for him. Frederick Wickenden died in 1918 at the age of ninety-three.

The original Frederick Wickenden adobe consisted of three rooms in a row. It was remodeled about 1880 to include a second story and was then cloaked in a Victorian garb of wood siding and jig-saw ornament.

THE DANIEL HILL ADOBE

The sketch depicts this old adobe as it may have appeared in the 1860's. It was drawn from the recollection of pioneers and a water-color painting in the possession of Mrs. James G. Williams.

THE DANIEL HILL ADOBE

THE DANIEL HILL ADOBE AT GOLETA

Los Cocheros is the name given to about 2000 acres of broad, rich bottom-land near Goleta. It is about eight miles northwest of the courthouse in Santa Barbara and on La Patera Lane, a quarter of a mile north of U. S. Highway 101. It was a portion of Dos Pueblos Rancho, conveyed to Nicholas A. Den through a Mexican grant by Governor Alvarado under date of April 18, 1842.

As early as 1830 Daniel Hill was interested in this region. It was then that a schooner was built and launched in a bay not far from this property. The Spanish word for schooner, **goleta**, furnished the name for the grant adjoining Los Cocheros on the east, La Goleta, which was given to Daniel Hill by Governor Pio Pico in 1846. It is probable that Daniel Hill had a hand in building the schooner. Another schooner was wrecked, at an early date, and washed ashore in this bay, and gave the name Goleta double significance.

Los Cocheros was included in that portion of Dos Pueblos grant obtained by Nicholas A. Den, Hill's son-in-law. Hill later sold 1300 acres to another son-in-law, Thomas Wallace More. In the middle seventies More built the first wharf in Goleta, (long since disappeared) the spot now bearing the designation of More's Landing. It is of interest to note that More's daughter, Martha More, born in the Daniel Hill adobe house at Los Cocheros, was the mother of the Santa Barbara publisher, Thomas M. Storke. Thomas Wallace More was murdered in 1877, shot while attempting to carry a harness from the barn which his assailants had set on fire.

Near More's Landing are extensive asphalt beds from which early residents of Santa Barbara and that vicinity procured material to waterproof their flat-roofed adobes and also to stabilize their dirt floors. In 1867, 2000 tons of this asphalt seepage were shipped to San Francisco. O. H. O'Niel, who from 1890 to 1893 served as wharfinger at More's Landing, recalls that large quantities of this asphalt were shipped from there.

Daniel Hill was born in Billerica, Massachusetts, in 1799 and came to California in 1823 as first officer of the sailing vessel "Rover," which was engaged in trade with the Sandwich Islands. In 1825 the young Yankee married Senorita Rafaela Luisa Ortega, a daughter of Jose Vicente Ortega, who was a son of Jose Maria Ortega, the son of Captain Jose Francisco Ortega of old Spanish **sangre azul.** That first Ortega came to San Diego in 1769 as **comandante** of the soldiers of Spain, and in 1782 cooperated with

Governor Felipe de Neve and the Padre Presidente, Junipero Serra, in establishing the Presidio Real at Santa Barbara and was its first **comandante**. Rafaela Ortega de Hill was mentioned by Alfred Robinson, who visited at the first Hill home in Santa Barbara and made this brief observation in his "Life in California":

"Supper was soon announced, when we had the pleasure of seeing the lady of the house, a fine healthy-looking female, with splendid eyes and beautiful black hair; but she said little and soon retired with her children."

The fourteen children born to Daniel Hill and Rafaela Luisa Ortega de Hill were: Rosa, who married Nicholas A. Den; Josefa, who married Dr. Alexander S. Taylor; Susana, who married T. Wallace More; Maria Antonia, who married Dr. Owen H. O'Niel; Adelade, who married E. Scollan; Lucrecia, who died young; and Helena. The sons were: Vicente, Jose Marcia, Juan, Tomas, Ramon, Enrique and Daniel.

The first home built by Daniel Hill was the historic old adobe still standing at 11 East Carrillo Street in Santa Barbara and popularly called the Carrillo Adobe. This early home of Daniel Hill has the distinction of having sheltered Mrs. Holmes, the first American woman resident of Santa Barbara. She came from the East to be under Hill's care until the arrival of her husband, Captain Holmes. Here she received the news of her husband's death at sea. There was nothing for her to do but remain in the Hill home until suitable passage for her return trip could be arranged. But before the plans for the trip were completed, she was married, under Daniel Hill's protection, to Thomas Oliver Larkin, who had been a fellow-passenger on her trip West. Mrs. Thomas Oliver Larkin was truly the pioneer New England woman of California.

In the forties Daniel Hill built his more pretentious home at Goleta. This was not on La Goleta grant but on the Cocheros property owned by Nicholas A. Den and sold to Daniel Hill. The cattle industry was then the order of the day and vaqueros were numerous. Planting and tilling did not appeal to Hill. This venerable adobe house that he built at Los Cocheros is in many respects an innovation in the adobe building practices of the period. Its floor plan differs from the typical one-story single row of rooms sometimes designed in a U-shape around a patio. The adobe portion of Los Cocheros house is in the shape of a rectangle thirty by sixty feet, with two rows of rooms and a heavy adobe partition through its center. This has appreciably strengthened the construction. A typical open corridor extends across the south facade.

Because of the loss of cattle through the drought of the sixties, Daniel Hill became land-poor. He died in 1865 and the property went to his widow, who later married George Center, who became the owner of the old homestead on her death. The dormer windows and present second-story rooms were added at a later date.

In 1901 James G. Williams acquired this property. Finding the adobe greatly in need of repairs, for the southwest wall had fallen out, he modernized the structure and in 1904 brought his bride here to establish their home. It was during this remodeling that the mast of a schooner that had served as the main ridge pole was removed and milled lumber put in its place. Probably this mast was salvaged from the schooner that had been wrecked in the bay. The small windows on the south facade of the house were replaced by French doors and a coat of heavy wooden siding was placed over the entire adobe on its exterior. The interior, too, was done over in accordance with the vogue of the early part of the century. Subsequently changes and additions were made as required. The old house continues to be a comfortable, livable home.

SANTA ROSA RANCHO ADOBE

This fine old adobe has been allowed
to reach a state of dilapidation. It
was once the hospitable home of the
Cota family, then of the Cooper
family, and later of the Carteri
family.

SANTA ROSA RANCHO ADOBE

THE COTA ADOBE ON SANTA ROSA RANCHO

In 1839 the Santa Rosa Rancho, consisting of three and a half Spanish leagues, was a Mexican grant to Francisco Cota. This grant, which is located about eleven miles east of the present town of Lompoc, was largely used by its original owner as grazing lands for vast herds of cattle and bands of sheep. Shepherds lived with their flocks. During shearing time as many as three dozen shearers were employed. According to present standards of measurement the estate consisted of about 17,000 acres.

About 1848 the Santa Rosa Rancho adobe house, which still stands, was built by Don Maria de Jesus Olivera de Cota. The homestead, built of sun-dried adobe blocks, is magnificently located on a knoll, overlooking the holdings. An orchard and shade trees were planted around it. The commodious house with its full-length veranda is, even in its present state of dilapidation, one of the most imposing of the early ranch houses extant in California. Some of its exterior adobe walls that sprang from the soil on the spot are four feet in thickness. Its heavy timber beams are said to have been transported there from a distance by Indians. The house was designed in the shape of a letter U. The **sala** and dining room are on the east, shaded by a full-length veranda. The bedrooms and smaller rooms are in the north wing. The kitchen was added later. It was at first the custom for Spanish-Californians to cook in the courtyard. The rooms were unceiled, exposing the heavy timbers of the roof construction. Large candle and oil chandeliers hung from the center beams. Here a corner fireplace is a unique example of early fireplace design quite rare in this Spanish-California architecture. The millwork and wood trim and shutters for the windows indicate that such refinements came from one of the early planing mills that furnished similar details for some of the best houses in Santa Barbara in the early fifties.

In 1868 the rancho was purchased by Joseph W. Cooper, and the Cota family moved to Santa Barbara to live. In the nineties the estate was leased to Leon Carteri, a Frenchman who had married Matilde Foxen, a daughter of William Domingo (Benjamin) Foxen and Eduarda Osuna Foxen. Their daughter, Leontine Carteri Verhelle, vividly recalls childhood days at the Santa Rosa Rancho in the "gay nineties," when the art of hospitality and gracious living was still practiced in this historic house. It was then that Senor Leon ran 30,000 head of sheep and 3000 head of cattle. Servants, vaqueros, and an accomplished governess, who had come directly from Ireland, added color to the scenes which still remained pastoral on this secluded **rancho.** Here the people sang a great deal, danced when they wished, and got from life the natural joys of living.

In 1912 the Cooper family, who still owned the property and had been occupying the house subsequent to the Carteri tenancy, took up their residence at Rancho la Vina and the old homestead was left vacant.

In 1938 this memorable landmark was offered as a gift to Santa Barbara County by the California Lands Incorporated. The offer was contingent on an adequate and authentic restoration of the adobe house. The offer, unfortunately, was declined and an opportunity lost to acquire and preserve for posterity an historical landmark.

THE BUENAVENTURO PICO HOUSE

The old adobe home of Buenaventuro Pico and his wife Anita Pico was built before 1850. A few yards to the southwest of it on the spot where the Lobero Hotel now stands, stood the commodious Cota House which was the home of Francisco Cota's family after they moved to Santa Barbara from the Santa Rosa Rancho. The Pico house was sold to Dr. Knox and became the property of his daughter, Mrs. Gertrude Knox Felly. It is a typical small adobe of the early period, with little architectural or historical significance and is completely hidden from view by the commercial buildings that surround it.

THE GASPAR ORENA ADOBE

The rear view of this house shows
a patio reminiscent of old Spain.
The dormer window, a feature so
common to our Eastern Colonial
architecture, is also a detail not uncommon in Andalusia. The house,
when viewed from its patio, appears as in the drawing.

THE GASPAR ORENA ADOBE

THE GASPAR ORENA ADOBES

Don Gaspar Eugenio de Orena Gomez de Escaudon was born in northern Spain in 1824 and studied medicine in that kingdom before coming to California in 1842. After becoming established in Santa Barbara, Don Gaspar married Dona Maria Antonia de la Guerra Lataillade, the widow of Cesareo Lataillade, who was the daughter of Don Jose Antonio Julian de la Guerra y Noriega, the beloved **comandante** of Santa Barbara's presidio in the early part of the century.

The east portion of El Adobe Orena was built in 1849 by Don Jose de la Guerra as a storehouse for merchandise purchased from ships that anchored in the harbor and was later sold to Don Gaspar Orena. In 1858 Don Gaspar built the story-and-a-half portion, and most of the thirteen children of Dona Maria were born in the Orena adobe. The family had previously lived on State Street, but that house burned down. In the spring and summer they lived at La Espada, one of Don Gaspar's cattle ranches which was on the coast near what is now Surf.

The second part of the Orena house stands at a slight angle to the first part. It may be of interest that in keeping with the rules of California hospitality the door of the Orena house was always open, and to the family's surprise, one day a perfect stranger walked in, sat down at the piano (which was a rarity and one of the few in Santa Barbara) and played until he had satisfied his longing to touch a keyboard. This adobe was restored in 1921 under the direction of James Osborne Craig. Mr. Craig subsequently restored the de la Guerra adobe and created El Paseo, which utilizes an inner patio covered by a high canopy, as an open-air restaurant. A group of studios are gathered about it in a picturesque manner, forming a Street in Spain.

Both portions of the Orena adobe are now owned by a daughter of Don Gaspar, Mrs. James Rickard, who was born in this family home. The property is leased to R. L. Lewis, who has continued to restore and improve these adobes while retaining their early-California charm. Mr. Lewis' antique shop is a "must" in Santa Barbara. In reconstruction it was found that part of the foundation wall, to about three or four feet above grade, contained rocks and large stones laid in adobe mortar. The adobe brickwork began at this height. Some of the window panes were of blown glass of rather poor visibility. The eastern portion was used as a store after 1853 when Don Gaspar moved into the two buildings. These historic houses are located on the north side of De la Guerra Street between the de la Guerra homestead and Anacapa Street.

The front of the house is typical of its early-California proto-types, possessing a full-fronted porch which extends as a covered passageway over the present sidewalk. Its tile roof and the three dormer windows that lead from the loft, one on the front and two on the rear, add distinction to its simple architecture. Dormer windows, which have come to be thought of as purely Eastern-Colonial in their derivation, have ample precedent in the houses of old Spain.

THE CORDERO ADOBE No. 1

The Cordero adobe No. 1 has
been given the name **Casa de
Cuatro Puerta,** The House
with Four Doors, by its owners, who have restored it
with an air of early Santa
Barbara.

THE CORDERO ADOBE No. 1

THE CORDERO ADOBES

The Cordero Adobe No. 1 is situated behind a small store at the northeast corner of Garden and East Canon Perdido Streets, at 906 Garden Street. The date of its construction is not known, and there seem to be no significant historical facts connected with it. Report has it that the house may have been built as early as 1828 by Refugio Cordero. Others state that it was built in 1850 by Jose Cordero. One of its occupants, Senorita Cordero married a Wilson and lived there for many years. At first, the house was one large adobe room. Later, it was divided into two rooms by a wooden partition. A wood-frame lean-to was added. In 1940 it stood in a dilapidated condition, serving for scarcely more than a tin-can dump for the neighborhood. The wood-siding that encased the adobe portion through the years has done much to preserve it.

The Cordero adobe No. 1 came again into its own through its sympathetic restoration by Mrs. Lyla M. Harcoff. In spite of discouraging advice she purchased the place during World War II, removed the center partition and the dilapidated, termite-eaten lean-to and added a hall, modern bath and kitchen. Mrs. Harcoff has made a charming cottage of the old adobe, having restored it in the spirit of the early days of Santa Barbara.

Mr. and Mrs. Floyd M. Nalley acquired the property in 1946 and have landscaped it most effectively, using grape-stake fences for privacy, and incorporating a barbecue, and sun terrace flanked by a rock wall. They call the place "Casa de Cuatro Puerta", or house of four doors.

The Cordero adobe No. 2 is located at 304 East Carrillo Street. The two adobe rooms of this house have been incorporated in a wood-frame house. It is reported that Juan Cordero brought his bride to this adobe house in 1850. No particular historical significence is attached to it.

THE VICENTE ORTEGA ADOBE

This house remodeled in the
days when Yankee millwork
became the fashion, is mainly constructed of adobe, but
has one end and a projected
wing of wood-frame con-
struction. The porch columns
and their jig-saw corbels are
delicately executed and give
a quaint Victorian effect.

THE VICENTE ORTEGA ADOBE

THE VICENTE ORTEGA ADOBE

The Vicente Ortega adobe, which was built by the Ortega brothers, Pedro and Jose, in the late 1840's or the early 1850's, is a convincing heirloom. Its builders were descendants of Captain Jose Francisco Ortega, the founder of Santa Barbara, who established the Presidio Real in 1782. They called their **rancho** the Arroyo Hondo, by which name Santa Barbarans still know it.

Although motorists may get a fleeting glimpse of the old adobe, deep in a ravine on the inland side of Highway 101 which parallels the ocean, at a place about thirty miles north of Santa Barbara, it formerly held greater prominence in relationship to the old stage road that passed its door, and wound a tortuous way up the canyon's side. This was before the railroad, and later the highway, bridged the ravine for the benefit of puffing locomotives and endless lines of automobiles.

It was in those days that this Ortega house was a regular stop, where stage passengers ate and refreshed themselves for the remainder of the journey from Santa Barbara northward towards the village of Lompoc.

Vicente Ortega tells that his grandfather, Pedro Ortega, has recounted how an occasional bandit came that way, as did the famous outlaw, Joaquin Murietta, on one occasion, when he demanded an exchange of horses and food.

The Ortega adobe has never been remodeled to any extent, although a small frame bedroom and a shed at the rear were added years ago.

Pedro Ortega, one of the brothers who built the house, had four sons: Fernando, Jose, Andrew and Alfred; and four daughters: Josie, Madalina, Tonia and Micaela, all born in this adobe.

By its escape from modernization, the aging walls of its seven adobe rooms and the frame portions that make up the sturdy structure, have retained a forthright integrity seldom found in adobe houses which have undergone extensive restoration.

It is a rare gem, in a perfect setting.

THE EDUARDO DE LA CUESTA ADOBE

This hospitable homestead
near Buellton, built by Doctor Ramon de la Cuesta, is
a prized landmark of the
early days of Santa Barbara
County. The sketch shows
the south side of the house.

THE EDUARDO DE LA CUESTA ADOBE

CULLIMORE

THE EDUARDO DE LA CUESTA ADOBE

In 1853 Doctor Ramon de la Cuesta and his wife Micaela Cota de la Cuesta built this adobe homestead, which still stands on the south bank of the Santa Ynez River near the town of Buellton on Highway 101. The house was built under great difficulties, as there were no roads and the lumber that was not hewn on the place had to be brought over Gaviota Pass on the heads of oxen, for ox-carts could not come through. This home has thirteen rooms, and stands much as it did when first built.

Doctor de la Cuesta, born in Spain, came to California in 1849. In 1851 he purchased Rancho La Vega, which consisted of 8,000 acres and was formerly a part of Rancho Najoque, owned by Raimundo Carrillo, who was the founder of the Carrillo family in California. It was there he built his adobe home.

The main entrance consists of a pair of doors. This was often the case in the early houses. For security a wooden bar was placed on the inside. The double-hung windows, associated with Eastern-Colonial precedent, which are shown in the accompanying sketch, were much in vogue in California about a century ago, and with some improvements are still in fashion today. A large room at the rear of the house was originally an open court.

The foundations of this house are of field stone laid in adobe mortar. The adobe walls are plastered inside and out. The ceilings are of pine boards 1" x 4" tongue-and-groove, beaded at the joints. The roof is covered with shingles. The outside of the adobe walls of the rear portion, which are not sheltered by the porch roof, is clapboarded to give protection from the elements.

On the exterior, the sash, doors, shutters and trim are painted a light green. All other exterior woodwork is painted white.

During the years, many celebrated people have sojourned here. The late Eduardo de la Cuesta, who with his family occupied the old homestead for many years, was a son of Ramon and Micaela Cota de la Cuesta. His wife was Eleva de la Cuesta, a great-granddaughter of Carlos Antonio Carrillo, and a granddaughter of Captain William Dana, a Yankee pioneer of San Luis Obispo County.

The de la Cuesta adobe has for almost a century served well its purpose of comfortable living and still does. Its back-to-earth simplicity of design and construction give it an ageless quality that is its outstanding characteristic. Here the adobe style, literally growing out of the soil, did not go far afield for any of the materials of construction. It is a genuine embodiment of a building material used in conformity to its time.

THE DEN ADOBE

The house where Katherine Den Bell was born was demolished in 1886. It was built by her father, Nicholas Agustus Den, a physician who came to California in 1836 from Ireland and married a daughter of Daniel Hill. The Den house stood on the north side of Figueroa between Anacapa and State Streets and was a large, square, one-story building, shinge-roofed, with broad porches supported by heavy square pillars that rested on stone bases. These porches were on the front and rear. The windows were large, broad and deep, and had wooden shutters. The front door was wide and massive, with narrow glass lights on each side. A hall ran through the center with a glass door opening onto the rear porch. The **sala** and dining room were on opposite sides of the hall and facing the street. The bedrooms were at the rear, opening into the other rooms and also into the hall. There is no vestige of this house today.

CAPTAIN TRUSSELL'S ADOBE

In 1854 Captain Trussell, a
Maine Yankee, built this
adobe, achieving an Eastern
Colonial aspect. It is a prized
landmark of Santa Barbara.

THE CAPTAIN TRUSSELL ADOBE

CAPTAIN TRUSSELL'S ADOBE

The Trussell adobe house at 412 West Montecito Street stands as a monument to its builder, Captain Horatio Gates Trussell. He was named for General Horatio Gates of General George Washington's army. Captain Trussell, born in Orland, Maine, at the age of twenty-one commanded a clipper ship which sailed out of Boston in the 1840's. He had sailed in the Liverpool brig "Elizabeth" in 1837, was first officer of the "America" out of Portsmouth, N. H. in 1846, and was appointed chief master of the ship "Sea Lion" at Havre, France (date unknown). He came to California in the 1850's on the first steamboat to enter Santa Barbara harbor. He married Ramona Burke of Santa Barbara.

The "Winfield Scott," en route from San Francisco to Panama laden with homeward-bound gold-seekers and their gold-dust, was wrecked in 1853 on Anacapa Island off the Santa Barbara coast. Captan Kimberly, who found the wreck deserted but full of the finest foods and luxuries, like Robinson Crusoe succeeded in salvaging much of its cargo before the ship broke up. Most of the timber portions of the Trussell adobe house were from the wreck of the "Winfield Scott." It was in 1854 that Captain Trussell incorporated these timbers in his Santa Barbara adobe house, which, when it was built, had a clear view of the channel. As a lad he had been trained in ship carpentry, and the results of this apprenticeship served him well when it came to the actual carpenter-work involved in framing the roof and floor, and door and window openings, which still display remarkable craftsmanship.

Being a Maine Yankee, steeped in the building traditions of that section, the captain could hardly have been expected to build himself a Spanish-California house, even on the Pacific slope. His house, although the central portion is of sun-dried adobe bricks laid after the prevailing California mode, reflects an Eastern-Colonial reserve in archtiectural line and detail that identify it with that period of transition in California when adobe construction was being superseded by wood-frame construction. The wings were of wood, and the shingle roof was one of the first in Santa Barbara. Horatio Trussell was a practical man and displayed in his house a logical use of available materials together with an avoidance of unnecessary ornamentation. This has given to the Trussell house a completely honest expression which is always the basis of good architecture. Several brass thresholds salvaged from the shipwreck are still in use under the old doors. Another reminder of

Captain Trussell's occupancy of the place is the largest cork oak tree in the United States. It was started from an acron brought from Washington, D. C., and planted by the captain in 1857. The tree is now dead, but still stands.

A room called "Peggy Stuart's" room, is in the southwest corner of the old adobe portion of the house. Peggy Stuart was the great-grandmother of the present generation of Trussells. Upon the reveal of the west doorway leading from this room to a boarded-in porch there has been preserved a small mural in black and white depicting a ship in full sail. This drawing was made by Mrs. Harlow Estes, the writer, who sketched it at a tender age. It will be recalled that Mrs. Estes, now of Boston, was the winner in 1939 of a $10,000 award for her book "Hildrith." Kate Douglas Wiggin also spent many happy days in this house as the guest of its owner, the late Mrs. Charlotte Bagg.

After occupying the chaste white adobe for nearly twenty years and establishing his family there, the captain built the present Trussell home, and the adobe passed from Trussell to Herman Eddy and subsequently was purchased in 1881 by a Santa Barbara public school teacher, Miss Sarah Winchester. It was later acquired by her brother, Doctor Robert F. Winchester and then by the doctor's sister, Mrs. Charlotte Bagg. Mrs. Bagg's daughter, Mrs. John Russell Hastings, now owns the place.

The furnishings of the Trussell adobe possess a flavor of old and appropriate selection that harmonizes with the gentility pervading it. A marine painting in oil, "Going Out to Sea," and a ship model of the brig "Pilgrim" are prized pieces acquired by Doctor Winchester. The painting was done by Captain Frank Thompson, a nephew of Captain Frank Thompson of the brig "Pilgrim," whom Dana describes in his "Two Years before the Mast." An occasional gilt mirror, a deep-set oval picture frame, highboys and bookcases that were made for their places find a perfect setting here. A massive hand-carved bedroom set of maple gives distinction to one bedroom. This set was a wedding present to Mrs. Bagg about seventy-five years ago and was brought around the Horn from Detroit, Michican, to California. In this adobe there is a mahogany square-backed chair from Dobbs Ferry Tavern, of the sort often put together in a pair to make a bed. As George Washington frequently visited the tavern it is not an unreasonable assumption that the general slept in it.

Although not dating back to the Spanish or Mexican era, this historic adobe, typical of the Yankee occupancy, is an authentic landmark and prized heirloom of the early fifties in Santa Barbara.

Through the generosity of the present owner of the Trussell adobe, Mrs. John Russel Hastings, the Santa Barbara Historical Museum was established in this historic house in 1943.

THE ALEXIS GODEY ADOBE

This old adobe ranch house
is rapidly passing into a state
of ruin.

THE ALEXIS GODEY ADOBE IN CUYAMA VALLEY

THE ALEXIS GODEY ADOBE IN CUYAMA VALLEY

The Alexis Godey house, in partial ruin, still stands on a knoll in the upper Cuyama Valley in Santa Barbara County near the Kern County line. The house, with a porch the full length, is typical of the long and narrow California houses. Some of the original timbers in the Godey adobe, part of which was built during the time Fort Tejon in Kern County was under construction, probably came from the sawmill that furnished much of the rough lumber for the fort. It was common gossip that a considerable amount of the lumber milled for the fort found its way to the surrounding ranchos. It has been reported that this was one of the reasons that the mill was moved nearer the fort and the logs hauled there to be sawed. The two original rooms at the east end had roof-trusses formed of poles with the bark peeled off. The bottom chords of these trusses have been sawed out, leaving the adobe walls to resist all of the roof thrust. In the later additions, rough-sawn lumber similar to that used at Fort Tejon, was used. In the board-and-batten addition the battens were cut in a pattern typical of millwork turned out in planing mills of California in the fifties.

In 1847, Cesareo Arnaud Lataillade and his wife, Maria Antonia de la Guerra de Carrillo of Santa Barbara, acquired title from Mexico to the Cuyama Ranchos, but in 1852 there were difficulties in establishing the legality of the grant, and as a result of the refusal of its title to the original owners, Alexis Godey settled upon it, and by the right of possession raised cattle there. He relinquished it to the Lataillade heirs when, by a special act of Congress, they were able to perfect their title in 1872. Although Alexis Godey had several common-law wives during his career, it is quite probable that the mistress of the Godey home in Cuyama was the first official one. His marriage to Maria Antonia Coronel, of a prominent Los Angeles family, was celebrated in Los Angeles. The bride's father, Ignacio Coronel, was the first schoolmaster in Los Angeles. On the day of the wedding the party dined at the Andres Pico adobe house in San Fernando and then continued on toward their new home in Cuyama Valley. The young wife was a beautiful, refined, and well-educated woman, entirely unsuited to life on the rancho or marriage to a man with Alexis Godey's habits. Their marriage ended in a separation and a financial settlement. Soon after this, Godey lost the Cuyama property to Mrs. Orena.

In recent years there has developed a legend that Alexis Godey was responsible for a massacre by poisoning of forty Indians in the

Cuyama Valley. The origin of this story has been traced to an article appearing in a Los Angeles publication in 1935. The story seems to be entirely without foundation and has been branded as false by many of the pioneers who knew Godey and the Cuyama Valley. F. F. Latta, a writer of Kern County and San Joaquin Valley history, in a pamphlet, "Alexis Godey," presents considerable evidence to disprove the story of the massacre.

Helen S. Giffen, in collaboration with Arthur Woodward in "The Story of El Tejon," states that in the early fifties Alexis Godey received several consignments of cattle from the federal government, intended for the Indians, but that they were appropriated by Godey for his own uses and were sold to miners. Misappropriation of government property in those days was not uncommon and not considered a serious crime.

THE MARIA ROMERO LOPEZ ADOBE

This ghostly ruin for many
years stood forlorn on the
center of a city block in the
residential section of Santa
Barbara. The roof has been
removed and the walls are
rapidly crumbling.

THE MARIA ROMERO LOPEZ ADOBE

THE MARIA ROMERO LOPEZ ADOBE

On March 8, 1855 Maria Romero Lopez acquired title to block 137 in Santa Barbara, bounded by the present streets of Figueroa, Olive, Carrillo and Laguna. Here he built his adobe house, of which only part of two crumbling walls of one room remain. It had stood there neglected for more than forty years, and then the roof was removed and the disintigration of the walls began. This adobe remained in the Lopez family for many years and then passed to to the Gonzales family. Gregorio Lopez, a prominent citizen and close friend of Nicholas A. Den, died there in the seventies. Steven T. Valenzuela recalled having participated in the funeral cortege as one of the candle-bearers when the body of Gregorio Lopez was removed in state from the old family adobe. In 1874 Jose Lopez lost the title for non-payment of taxes, and it became the property of M. Dupry. In 1880 it belonged to Cayetano Gonzales and Maria de la Luz Oliveria Gonzales.

"Old-timers" recall this adobe as a large house located on a commanding hill overlooking the ocean in the distance. It consisted of rooms opening on a long open corridor on its northerly facade. The house was famous for its lavish entertainment, barbecues and dances when it was the home of Gregorio Lopez, who was also the possessor of extensive ranch holdings. This property passed to the ownership of Robert L. Foxen, a son of Salvador Foxen.

THE BIRABENT ADOBE HOUSE

This house was built in the
late 1850's. Part of it was
constructed of adobe bricks
from the presidio's enclosure
walls. It is now cloaked by a
sheathing o f clapboards
which obscures its adobe construction.

THE BIRABENT ADOBE HOUSE

THE BIRABENT ADOBE HOUSE

Senora Lorenza Ordaz de Rochin was a fourth-generation niece of Captain Jose Francisco Ortega, one of the founders and the first **comandante** of the Presido Real, established in 1782 at Santa Barbara. Senora Rochin was born at San Gabriel Mission in 1832 and came to live in Santa Barbara in 1848. In 1856 she acquired a piece of property located within the old presidio confines. This plot, two hundred and fifty by one hundred and twenty feet, was the first part of the presidio property to be sold. The purchase price was $50. The house that Senora Rochin caused to be built on this lot still stands at 820 Santa Barbara Street and has remained in the possession of the family of the original builder for the past ninety years. Its present owners are Mr. and Mrs. Frank L. Birabent, Mrs. Birabent being a daughter of Senora Lorenza Ordaz de Rochin and born in Santa Barbara in 1864.

It is interesting to note that when Soledad Rochin (Mrs. Frank L. Birabent) was about eight years old, she lived on the ranch which her parents had rented and which included La Purisima Mission near Lompoc. The mission was not then used as a church but was occupied by the Rochin family as their residence. Mrs. Birabent recalls that the vestments and appointments of the church were still there at that time.

Jean Marie Birabent, a Frenchman, came to Santa Barbara County in 1860 to take charge of Las Cruces Rancho. In 1861 he married Maria Antonia Ortega. A son of this union, Frank L. Birabent, married Soledad Rochin, the daughter of Senora Rochin. Their wedding was solemnized in 1890, in "Our Lady of Sorrow" at the corner of State and Figueroa Streets. The wedding festivities took place in the Rochin adobe house.

This house was built on the inside of the presidio enclosure, whose walls were seven feet thick and twelve feet high. The Sloyd School was subsequently built adjacent to it on the other side of the wall. The house was constructed largely of adobe bricks from the ruins of some of the old presidio rooms originally built against this wall. There were also enough of the square floor tiles from these rooms to pave the floor of one of the three rooms in the Rochin house. Later, rooms were added at the rear. Today, the house has been remodeled into two apartments. The true character of the Rochin adobe is now completely concealed under its exterior of wood siding. It is only by entering the house that the adobe character is discerned, although its full-fronted porch and the general exterior lines correspond to the typical architectural forms of adobe houses built in the fifties.

ADOBE HOUSE OF JOSEFA VALDEZ DE GANNON

This small adobe, which originally consisted of but one
room, was built in 1859 for the
the widow Gannon. It is
rapidly b e i n g encroached
upon by business property.

ADOBE HOUSE OF JOSEFA DE GANNON

THE JOSEFA VALDEZ DE GANNON ADOBE

Josefa Valdez Gannon de Martinez, the mother of Senora Alfreda Ruiz, the present owner of the adobe house at 1022 Anacapa Street, caused her house to be built about 1859. This was during her widowhood from her first husband, Thomas Gannon. Gannon was an Irishman who had come around the Horn with Stevenson's regiment, which was mustered out of Mexican War service in California, and figures prominently in the records of Santa Barbara in the early fifties. Senora Gannon Martinez has often recounted to her children the whirlwind courtship of Thomas Gannon, who made his proposal of marriage on his first visit to the Casa Valdez. He was accepted by Senor Valdez, the young lady's father, and then the prospective bridegroom suggested that he seal the pact with a kiss on the lips of his fifteen-year-old fiancee. To this, paternal objection was voiced, as such a display of affection was only to take place after marriage. The wedding was solemnized as soon as the proper articles of finery could be procured from San Francisco.

About seven years later Senora Gannon was widowed. She had many valuable articles and jewelry that her husband had given her. These belongings she sold in order to purchase the property and have the adobe house built. It stands one block south of the County Courthouse. Indio Martin, the adobe expert of those days, is reputed to have superintended its construction. About 1862 Josefa Valdez de Gannon was married to Leandro Martinez. Mrs. Delfina Martinez Ruiz and Josefa Martinez, daughters of this marriage, inherited this property from their mother. Leandro Martinez had come to Califonia with Garcia Diego y Moreno, the first Bishop of California, and was for many years a cook for the padres at the mission.

The house at present consists of two adobe rooms and two of wood-frame. The improvement of Anacapa Street caused the removal of the old picket fence and the shortening of the yard. The large rear yard and garden, however, retain their old-time aspect.

THE MERIDIAN ADOBE

The Meridian adobe, at 114 East De la Guerra Street, is said to have been the old Lugo home and was one of the adobes which was moved back when the street was widened. It was the first office of the Plans and Planting Committee, in 1922. Meridian was the name given to the whole development when Bernard Hoffman purchased it and added studios to the property. A. C. Postel later acquired it and occupied the adjoining addition as his residence until 1947.

Monsieure and Madame Raoul de Malleville operate an attractive restaurant—Chanteclair—in this old adobe.

THE WILLIAM DOVER ADOBE

This adobe is of uncertain age, but
William Dover remodeled it in the
early 1860's and since then it has
been known as the William Dover
Adobe.

THE WILLIAM DOVER ADOBE

THE WILLIAM DOVER ADOBE

This small house, located at 725 Yanonali Street in Santa Barbara, was at one time the house of William Dover, a young English seaman who came to America around Cape Horn when but eighteen years old. A son, the late Joe Dover, has stated that his father set sail in 1845 and beached his ship because of a leak, in front of Burton's Mound, where the vessel broke up. Edward Bodie and William Pratt were also on the ship. The pilot house was salvaged and brought to a spot near the de la Guerra gardens to be used as a hunting camp. Later it was a chicken house on the site of the present city hall. With Captain Kimberly, Dover then became part owner of a schooner and went into the business of hunting otter and selling the pelts. They made their headquarters on Anacapa island. In 1860 he was granted a license to operate a sloop, "The Hamilton," out of San Diego.

In July, 1867, William Dover was given citizenship in the United States. The following year he acquired a parcel of land in the town of Santa Barbara. This property was bounded on the north by Nopal Street, on the south by Quarantina Street, on the east by Yanonali Street and on the west by Montecito Street. This naturalized Englishman married a native of Santa Barbara, Senorita Ynez Guevara, the lovely daughter of Canuto Guevara, of old Spanish stock. William Dover brought his bride to the adobe house that stood on his newly-acquired land. Here he raised his family.

This same property had been in the possession of his wife's family before he bought it. In 1856 Mr. and Mrs. Francis Lewis deeded it to William Dover. Mrs. Lewis, an older sister of Mrs. Dover, had lived there for some years. She has stated that Yanonali Street was then merely a trail that ran to the rear of the house, and was originally used by Chief Yanonali and his Indians as they went to and from the mission. John Dover, another son of William Dover, served as the inspiration for the title character in Margaret Cameron Lewis' historical novel "Johndover," the setting for which is laid in Santa Barbara and Montecito. Rosa, the youngest daughter of William Dover, became the wife of Tomas Olivera, and they occupied the old Dover adobe. Tomas Olivera's father, also named Tomas Olivera, was a grandson of Sergeant Ignacio Olivera, who was a member of the Padre Presidente Junipero Serra party when the Presidio Real of Santa Barbara was founded by Governor Felipe de Neve and Captain Jose Francisco Ortega, the first

comandante. Senor Tomas Olivera the First came from Los Angeles to Santa Maria with his first wife, Senora Valenzuela Olivera.

The Tequepis **rancho** was granted to Thomas Olivera, April 7, 1837, and transferred to Antonia Maria de Cota, his second wife, at a later date. It consisted of 9800 acres. Here Tomas Olivera the Second was born. The Oliveras built two adobe homes that stood near Santa Maria, one for themselves and one for the Ruiz family. The Olivera family mentioned here claims relationship to the Olvera family for which Olvera Street in Los Angeles is named. A slight corruption is evident in the spelling of the name, the Los Angeles branch having omitted the letter "i". It is also claimed that Juan de Dios Olivera (or Olvera), the son of Sergeant Ignacio Olivera, is the **Angelino** for whom Olvera Street was named.

The Dover property, with improvements thereon which included the original adobe house, was deeded to William Dover on March 21, 1868. The house then consisted of three adobe rooms in a row, with the **sala,** which contained a fireplace, occupying the center position. It is probable that the first floor was of packed earth as was the prevailing custom. Later, asphalt was brought in from Carpenteria and used for the floors of the house and the open corridor in front. The twenty-four-inch exterior adobe walls supported poles, which served as roof beams. On these beams, slender saplings were placed to form a ceiling. Upon this a mat of kelp rested, then a layer of earth, more kelp and more earth. This afforded a superior insulation against summer heat and some degree of resistance to winter rains. Its effectiveness in the rainy season was directly proportional to the number of layers of kelp and earth. The deep reveals on the inside of the window openings afforded an opportunity for shelves and window seats.

After the coming of the Yankees the interior was embellished with a New England type of milled woodwork, mouldings, and trim, all of which became typical of the details of the adobe style of architecture shortly after California's advent into the United States. William Dover built a room of wood construction on the east end of the house. The art of carpentry was well understood by Dover, as is evidenced by the finely-fitted joints, secured with wooden pegs, which are still a part of the construction. Some hand-forged nails were also used as fastenings. It is said that Ed Bodie, who was with William Dover on his ship, helped with the frame construction of the addition to the Dover house. Indio Martin

(Violin Martin) is reputed to have worked on the adobe portion.

A news item in the Santa Barbara weekly "Independent" of August 20, 1887, makes a statement to the effect that William Dover played an unexpected role in the celebration centering around the arrival of the first railroad train in Santa Barbara. Dover, having imbibed a little too freely, sat down to rest on a projecting cross-tie. The first train struck him, but he lived to see it pass again—in a soberer mood.

In 1925, prior to the earthquake of that year, only the **sala** of this adobe remained. It was then that its present owner, Tomas Olivera, and his wife, the late Rosa Dover Olivera, remodeled and added to the old structure, giving it the outward characteristics which it now possesses. The design, with its full-length porch, whose roof is supported by heavy posts capped by wooden corbels, is reminiscent of early California. The red-tile roof adds its note of color. A fitness to the Santa Barbara environment, together with a long service in supplying the domestic needs of the social order it represents, gives it a claim to distinction. The simplicity of line and absence of unnecessary ornamentation combine with a genuineness that is intrinsic to adobe construction.

THE BOTILLER ADOBE

This adobe house, located at 1023 Bath Street, was originally surrounded by its plot of land consisting of four city blocks. The property was acquired in 1843 by Pascual Botiller, a young Frenchman, who built upon it his two-story adobe house. Botiller raised grapes on these premises, as was the prevailing custom in that section of Santa Barbara. A small press and winery completed his equipment for wine-making. It was on account of the several vineyards in this vicinity that the name De la Vina was given to the street passing through them.

Botiller acquired another parcel of land bounded by Canon Perdido, Laguna, De la Guerra, and Garden Streets. On this land for many years he raised vegetables for the housewives of Santa Barbara. On foot, carrying his basket from house to house, he was a well known figure. It will be noted that his vegetable gardens were in a natural depression. Taking advantage of this terrain, he devised a miniature, dirt-lined reservoir on a high point of the premises and released water as necessary for irrigation during the dry summer months. This innovation was not without its drawbacks, as the waterhole proved a source of irresistible temptation to the boys of the neighborhood who, much against the gardener's wishes, made use of it as a swimming hole during his absence.

Upon Botiller's death, the homestead went to his widow, Feliciana Carlon Botiller. At Feliciana's death in 1888, it was inherited by her daughter, who had married Gerard Grand, a Parisian who came to Santa Barbara at the age of 19.

Family tradition recounts that a not-too-distant relative, Mlle. Botiller, was a trusted member of the entourage of the Emperor Maximilian. It has been passed down by word-of-mouth that this Botiller was entrusted with the crown jewels of Empress Carlotta.

The Botiller house is one of the few two-story adobes in Santa Barbara and consists of three adobe rooms on the first floor, although there are now additional frame portions extending to the rear. On the second floor there is one large room to which a winding stairway gives access from the **sala** or central downstairs room. Architecturally, there are no unusual or distinctive features to this old house. It is a sturdy structure, as is evidenced by the fact that, in spite of its two-story construction, it withstood the earthquake of 1925 without serious damage. Its details follow the patterns typical of the late Mexican and early Yankee period.

The Botiller adobe served its purpose well under the spell of Mexico and the United States.

The old structure, although linked with a cosmopolitan past, is now filled with a spirit that is truly American.

THE LORENZANO ADOBE HOUSE

This sketch, made from an old photograph in the possession of Mrs. A. J. Verhelle, shows the Lorenzano house, which, as early as the 1850's, stood on a spot between State Street and the De la Guerra Plaza.

THE LORENZANO ADOBE

THE LORENZANO ADOBE HOUSE

Although little known as an historic house in Santa Barbara, the Lorenzano adobe, which once stood on a spot in the rear of the place where the Johnston Cafeteria now stands, was typical of a style of architecture that developed in the early days of Santa Barbara and that was at its height when the Yankees took over and California was admitted to the Union.

The outstanding architectural feature of these old adobe houses is their lack of unnecessary ornamentation. Quite logically, it is a similar avoidance of unessentials that ear-marks the ultra-modern developments in domestic architecture, today. Perhaps this is one reason that the lines of these old adobe houses are much more appreciated today than in the early Yankee period when the pioneers from our eastern coast turned up their noses at California's Spanish houses.

THE FRANK KIRK ADOBE

There stands at 421 East Figueroa Street the adobe house once occupied by Frank W. Kirk, who married a daughter of the Arrellanes family and lived there in about 1875.

This house has but one room remaining of the original adobe—probably the **sala**. It is about 17 feet wide and 30 feet long, with a fireplace on the northeast wall near the corner of the room. The roof, which was once tile, has been replaced by shakes. The wide front door is of unusual interest, it being said that it was once used in the Old Mission. Its top is in two vertical glass panels of three panes each, and below there are two wood panels. This adobe sits well back from the street among large old trees and dense shrubbery. The exterior surface is unprotected by plaster or paint. In the west end is a large window with a pointed, triangular top which may indicate some special use. It may have been the setting for an improvised altar, used when the visiting priest made his rounds. The ceiling is new, having been placed there after the earthquake of 1925 and provided with heavy beams to strengthen the structure. In 1919 the property belonged to McCurdy, in 1922 to Jacob Goldstein, in 1925 to Chester Jordan and then to Frank Robinson. It is at present the property of Mr. and Mrs. John Gorham.

THE CARLOS COTA ADOBE

On the northwest corner of East Canon Perdido and Laguna Streets stands the adobe house of Carlos and Anne Goux Cota. The date of its construction is not known. It was once the property of Jose Jesus Calderon. In 1923, when the street was graded down, the quaint little adobe, with its typical front porch, was drastically remodeled and assumed its present form.

There are no historical incidents or architectural characteristics to distinguish it. However, in the olden days it ranked with many others as a small, pleasant place.

THE ONTIVEROS ADOBE

This commodious structure, now the prop-
perty of the Hancock holdings, located on
the Rosemary Ranch, stands deserted and
forlorn near the junction of the Sisquoc
and Cuyama rivers in Santa Maria Valley.

THE ONTIVEROS ADOBE

THE ONTIVEROS ADOBE

On la Brea or Rosemary Ranch, a part of the Hancock holdings, there stand the ruins of the once-pretentious Ontiveros adobe house. It is located about two miles from Geary and near the junction of the Sisquoc and Cuyama Rivers. This old adobe was built in about 1830 and served as the home for the Ontiveros family. It consists of six large rooms in a row, with porches on both sides. The fireplace and its wooden mantel are of especial interest, as are also the double doors and double-hung windows, muntined into six panes to each sash.

In the days when lavish hospitality was dispensed here, according to the recollection of pioneers, barbecues and fiestas were not uncommon. Then the out-of-doors oven or **horno** was adjacent to the kitchen. These beehive ovens were stoked with fuel, which was allowed to burn until it was thought that a desired temperature had been attained. Then the remaining fuel and the coals were raked out and the bread or meat put in to cook. The oven door was generally near the kitchen and the oven itself so located that the prevailing breeze carried the smoke in the direction of the lesser household activities.

THE PACKARD ADOBE

This old winery was once the center of
a grape-growing industry. It was also
the scene of an enterprise in growing silk-
worms.

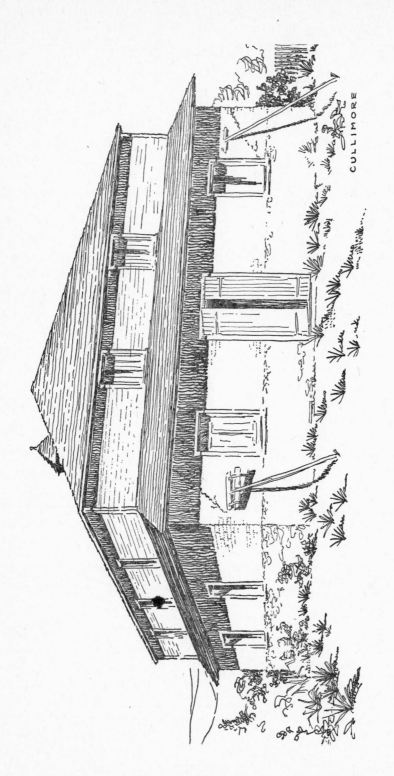

THE PACKARD ADOBE

CULLIMORE

THE PACKARD ADOBE

This building, which stands at 525 West Carrillo Street, was erected about 1865 as a winery. It was known in the early days as La Bodega or wine cellar, having been the center of a large vineyard and a considerable trade in wine made from grapes in the vicinity. The wine was exported to Europe under the name of "El Recodo," meaning "The Corner." Its original owner was Albert Packard, a Rhode Islander who arrived in California from Mazatlan about 1845 at the age of twenty-five and who lived in Santa Barbara for many years. He married a daughter of Mrs. Isaac Sparks, born in Bowdinham, Maine. Packard was a prosperous hunter of sea otter and was well known as a prominent lawyer, fruit-grower, vineyardist, and an extensive landowner, having at one time owned the Jesus Maria Rancho, formerly a part of the Santa Lucia Rancho, which was a Mexican grant.

The Packard adobe has a basement under the entire structure. The basement walls are of rock. The main floor is of heavy timber construction, and the rock walls continue to about six feet above the grade, where the adobe begins. The adobe walls extend for about eight feet, to the beams of the second floor. The third story is of clapboards. The adobe masonry work was poorly bonded at the corners. It separated in the earthquake of 1925. The timber work of the interior is exceptionally well built and is attributed to the hands and supervision of Captain Trussell, who was related to Albert Packard's wife. The original shingles still remain on the roof and are in remarkably good condition.

The winery took three years to build. The lumber came from Oregon by sailing vessel. After being thrown overboard in the bay it was washed ashore and then hauled by oxen to the building site. The laborers were mainly Indians. The equipment at the winery included a crushing machine and a wine press. The vats, which were about ten feet high, were shipped in shooks and put together, on the job, by a Frenchman, Pedro Dejame, or "Caracci" as he was known. "Colonel Pico" was the first major-domo, followed by Edward Breck, who was there for twenty-five years and who died at the age of ninety-one. A brandy or **aguardiente** distillery was also operated here. The brandy sold at $2.50 a gallon and the wine from 25c up, according to age.

It is of interest to note that the third story of **La Bodega** was once used for an experiment in the silk-worm industry, probably the first venture of its kind in the United States. Emil Goux was also interested in this. The original larvae were brought from Japan. Albert Packard planted many mulberry trees for their food, and a number of women were employed to cut the leaves for feeding. The industry failed to pay and was discontinued.

La Bodega passed to the possession of Arthur Gleave, a Santa Barbara florist.

THE DOCTOR SHAW ADOBE

This dilapidated, one-room adobe structure
is all that remains of the once well-appointed
home owned by Doctor Shaw of Los Alamos.

THE DOCTOR SHAW ADOBE

THE DOCTOR SHAW ADOBE

The adobe house that Doctor James B. Shaw built on La Laguna Rancho, a part of the Los Alamos grant, may have had several rooms. Only one and a loft, or half-story, over it remain. This room was at one time used as a kitchen, as the carpentry of a wooden sink testifies. The stairway to the loft is an interesting bit of carpentry. There is no particular architectural significance to this adobe.

Doctor Shaw was a well-educated English gentleman, who came to Santa Barbara in the 1870's and practiced medicine here. He acquired La Laguna Rancho and was responsible for the laying-out of the town of Los Alamos. The name Laguna, or lake, was given to the **rancho** on account of an artificial lake that formerly stood there, but which, it has been reported, ceased to exist when a cloudburst washed out the dam.

On his travels in his seagoing yacht, Dr. Shaw once visited the island of St. Helena and brought back from the tomb of Napoleon cuttings from a weeping-willow tree that overhung the French general's first burial place. There are two large weeping-willows near the Shaw adobe that are reported to have stemmed from this source. They stand on the bank of the former lake.

The Price Ranch, a part of the Doctor Shaw Ranch, including the old adobe, was purchased in 1921, and Mr. Price and his Parisian wife made their home in the wood-frame house adjacent to the Shaw adobe.

The adobe has recently been re-roofed with shingles, and serves as a store house.

THE GUADALUPE RANCHO HOUSE NO. 1

This house was built in 1850 on the property granted to Diego Olivera and Teodoro Arrellanes by the Mexican government in 1840.

GUADALUPE RANCHO HOUSE NO. 1

THE GUADALUPE RANCHO ADOBES

The Guadalupe Rancho was granted to Diego Olivera and Teodoro Arrellanes by the Mexican government on March 21, 1840. Diego Olivera was born in Santa Barbara about 1789 and throughout his life clung to the old Spanish ways in dress and manners. He once served as **alcalde**, or mayor, of Santa Barbara. Teodore Arrellanes was well-known and admired. The **rancho** consisted of about 30,000 acres of fertile soil.

In 1850 the first of the two **rancho** houses was built, and the second was constructed close by in 1868, by John B. Ward for his bride, a member of the Estudillo family.

The foundations of both of these houses are of field stone laid in adobe mortar. The adobe bricks of their walls are laid in similar mortar in which a small proportion of straw was included. The walls were then thinly plastered with more adobe mud, both inside and out. The interior was painted and the exterior whitewashed.

The floors of these houses are of pine planks, laid on joists which were placed flat and directly on the ground. The floors of the outside corridors were laid in the same manner. Only a small amount of this outside flooring, close to the adobe walls, still remains.

Their roofs are wood-framed and shingled, having an added distinction on account of their dormer windows.

Several of the corridor posts, which were neatly chamfered, have disappeared. The double-hung windows, so evidently of Yankee derivation, appear to be the original ones. In the second Guadalupe adobe, a door at the east has four heavily-moulded panels and four long, narrow pieces of glass in each of the two side-lights, and is flanked by a paneled pilaster on each side. The door opposite, at the west end of the hallway, is similar, except that there are no sidelights or pilasters. The interior doors are of the four-paneled variety so popular in the 1850's and 1860's. Although these doors and the windows were painted white, the other interior trim was grey.

In spite of the sad state of dilapidation in which these two old adobes stand, they seem to exhale into the small town of Guadalupe a breath of former gentility.

THE GUTIERREZ ADOBE

This old adobe is in a state of dilapidation.
Through lack of care and protection it is
slowly succumbing to the elements.

THE GUTIERREZ ADOBE

THE GUTIERREZ ADOBE

Situated on a small hill above Mission Canyon is the ruin of the adobe home of Senora Gutierrez, who married Pedro Ignacio, an Indian. The orchard which formerly surrounded it was called the Indian orchard.

Little is known about this now forlorn relic, or the people who lived there. It possesses no architectural significance.

THE HISTORIC ADOBE

The building at the right is the much-traveled Historic Adobe, which has several times been razed and the bricks reused to construct another adobe.

THE HISTORIC ADOBE

THE HISTORIC ADOBE

Adjacent to the Covarrubias adobe at 715 Santa Barbara Street is the one-story five-room house known as the "Historic Adobe." There are those who claim that it was built about 1836 at a position near the present corner of State and Carrillo Streets, for Concepcion Pico de Carrillo, sister of Pio Pico, the last of California's Mexican governors. It has also been known as General Fremont's headquarters, although this claim has not been substantiated. The building was removed brick by brick to Carrillo and Anacapa Streets, where it was used by the Museum of Natural History. In 1922 the adobe was again taken down and reconstructed in its present location by John R. Southworth. In 1925 the earthquake did no damage to this building. In 1938 the Historic Adobe and the Covarrubias adobe were sold to Rancheros Visitadores, and in 1941 both were restored and are now used as headquarters for this equestrian organization.

THE KIRK B. JOHNSON ADOBE

A view of the patio of the
Kirk B. Johnson a d o b e.
George Washington Smith
was the architect in charge
of its restoration.

THE KIRK B. JOHNSON ADOBE

THE KIRK B. JOHNSON ADOBE

The elaborately-rebuilt Tajiguas Rancho adobe belonging to Kirk B. Johnson was originally one of the several Ortega adobes that dotted the extensive holdings of the Ortega family. The original adobe that stood on this spot was built in about 1800, and in 1879 additions and improvements were made. Subsequently, the old house fell into ruin. In 1924 the architect, George Washington Smith, was commissioned to build the present structure. Using about two thirds of the original adobe bricks and most of the old roof tile, he has made of it one of the most attractive and outstanding adobes in California.

Although the present house does not actually extend back of the Johnson ownership of the **rancho,** it is the same in general dimensions as the old one, with the exception of the new wing and kitchen, which are a frame lean-to added to the old structure. The original part of the old adobe, built perhaps as early as 1800, consisted of four walls approximately twenty-four feet by forty-two feet and was divided into six rooms. An open-end **bodega,** or storage room for wine, meat and supplies, was probably added later to the original structure; this was followed by the frame building which was used as a kitchen. In 1879 the dining room, corresponding to the room later used by Mr. Johnson as his office, was completed by the Young family, who then owned the **rancho.**

The Tajiguas Rancho adobe is located about eighteen miles north of Santa Barbara, a few miles inland on a private road leading from Highway 101.

BIBLIOGRAPHY

BIBLIOGRAPHY

BOOKS

BANCROFT, HUBERT HOWE, **History of California.** 4 Vols.; San Francisco: L. A. Bancroft and Company, 1881-1888. Vol. I, 744 pp; Vol. II, 795 pp.; Vol. III, 792 pp.; Vol IV, 786 pp.

BELL, KATHERINE M., **Swinging the Censor.** Santa Barbara: Published by her children, 1931. 287 pp.

CAMERON, MARGARET, **Johndover.** New York: Harper and Brothers, (1923, 1924). 483 pp.

DANA, RICHARD HENRY, **Two Years Before the Mast.** Boston and New York: Houghton Mifflin Company, 1911. 554 pp.

GIFFEN, HELEN F., and ARTHUR WOODWARD, **The Story of El Tejon.** Los Angeles: Dawson's Book Shop, 1942. 146 pp.

HAWLEY, WALTER, **Early Days of Santa Barbara.** Santa Barbara: Osborne's Book Store, 1910. 105 pp.

HILL, LAWRENCE, and PARKS, MARION, **Santa Barbara—Tierra Adorada.** Los Angeles: Security-First National Bank, 1930. 113 pp.

MASON, JESSIE D., **History of Santa Barbara County.** Oakland, California: Thompson and West, 1883. 477 pp.

O'NEIL, OWEN H., editor, **History of Santa Barbara County.** Santa Barbara: Harold McLean Meier Publishing Company, 1939. 469 pp.

PHILLIPS, MICHAEL J., **History of Santa Barbara County.** 2 Vols.; Chicago: The S. J. Clarke Publishing Company, 1927. Vol. I, 464 pp.; Vol. II, 461 pp.

RENSCH, H. E. and RENSCH, E. G., **Historic Spots in California: The Southern Counties.** Stanford University Press, 1932. 267 pp.

Santa Barbara's Old Spanish Background. Santa Barbara: Chamber of Commerce, undated. 10 pp.

SOUTHWORTH, JOHN R., **Historic Adobes of Santa Barbara County.** Santa Barbara: Privately published, 1920. 28 pp.

STORKE, MRS. YDA ADDIS, **Santa Barbara, San Luis Obispo, and Ventura Counties.** Chicago: The Lewis Publishing Company, 1891. 677 pp.

W. P. A. PROJECT, **Santa Barbara, A Guide to the Channel City and Its Environs.** New York: Hastings House, 1941. 206 pp.

THESIS AND UNPUBLISHED ARTICLE

LANE, KATHLEEN R., **The Early History of Goleta.** Unpublished Master's thesis, The University of Southern California, Los Angeles, California, 1935.

NEWSPAPERS

Weekly Independent, Santa Barbara, August 20, 1887 (Dover).
Daily Press, Santa Barbara, December 24, 1881 (Trabucco).
Daily News, Santa Barbara, March 7, 1937 (Ramirez).
Daily News, Santa Barbara, March 21, 1937 (Miranda).
Daily Press, Santa Barbara, November 6, 1938 (Cota, Santa Rosa).
News-Press, Santa Barbara, June 18, 1942 (Yorba-Abadie).

PERSONAL INTERVIEWS AND WRITTEN STATEMENTS

MR. FRANK ARROQUI, August, 1942, one time occupant of the Masini adobe.

MRS. WALTER BENFIELD, manuscript relating to Benjamin Foxen, undated.

MR. AND MRS. FRANK L. BIRABENT, November 16, 1944, owners of Birabent adobe.

MRS. MERCEDES CARRIAGA, August, 1942, daughter of Bruno Orella.

MISS PEARL CHASE, June, 1942, August, 1942, November 6, 1944, April 12, 1948, Secretary of The Plans and Planting Committee of Santa Barbara.

MRS. CARLOS GOUX COTA, November 30, 1944, granddaughter of Emil Goux.

MISS AURORA COVARRUBIAS, November 20, 1944, granddaughter of Jose Maria Covarrubias.

MISS YNEZ DE LA CUESTA, September 6, 1944, daughter of Eduardo de la Cuesta.

MR. T. WILSON DIBBLEE, July, 1942, descendant of Don Jose de la Guerra.

MR. TOM DINSMORE, July, 1942, supervisor of Santa Barbara County, grandson of Bradbury T. Dinsmore, pioneer.

MRS. GERTRUDE KNOX FELLY, June, 1942, owner of Buenaventuro Pico adobe.

MR. JOSEPH FOXEN, July, 1942, descendant of Benjamin Foxen.

MRS. MARY E. FOXEN, December 2, 1944, pioneer.

MR. ARTHUR GLEAVE, June, 1942, owner of Packard adobe.

MRS. JOHN GORHAM, July, 1942, occupant of Kirk adobe.

MR JULIAN GOUX, August 6, 1942, grand nephew of Emil Goux.

MRS. GERARD GRAND, November 14, 1944, owner and occupant of Botiller adobe.

MRS. LYLA M. HARCOFF, March 30, 1948, restorer of Cordero Adobe.

MR. A. B. HARMER, July 3, 1942, son of Alexander Harmer, owner of Yorba-Abadie adobe.

MRS. JOHN HARTNETT, August, 1942, pioneer.

MRS. JOHN RUSSEL HASTINGS, November 5, 1944, secretary of the Santa Barbara Historical Museum, owner of the Captain Trussell adobe.

MISS HELEN HOSMER, December 6, 1944, daughter of Thomas Hosmer, pioneer.

MRS. MARIA JOSEFA MALO DE JANSSENS, June, 1942, pioneer.

MISS MARGARITE JANSSENS, August, 1942, pioneer.

MR. AND MRS. KIRK B. JOHNSON, September 30, 1944, owners of the Kirk B. Johnson adobe.

MRS. SERENA ORENA DE KOCH, February, 1943, daughter of Gaspar Orena, pioneer.

MRS. HARRY LAMB, December 20, 1944, sister of Mrs. Tomas Olivera.

MR. ROBERT L. LEWIS, January, 1943, restorer of Orena adobe.

MRS. HELENA MEYER, August, 1942, occupant of the Masini adobe.

MRS. J. N. MONK, June, 1942, daughter of Francisco Nardi, pioneer.

MR. AND MRS. F. M. NALLEY, March 26, 1948, owner of Cordero Adobe No. 1.

MR. FRANCISCO NARDI, July, 1942, pioneer.

MR. TOMAS OLIVERA, June, 1942, occupant of the William Dover adobe.

MR. OWEN H. O'NEIL, November 15, 1944, descendant of Captain Jose Francisco Ortega.

MR. AND MRS. JAMES ORD, June 12, 1942, pioneers.

MR. AND MRS. VICENTE ORTEGA, November 6, 1944, owners of the Ortega adobe.

MR. AND MRS. O. S. PRICE, January 8, 1945, owners of part of the Doctor Shaw ranch.

MISS DELFINA M. RUIZ, November 13, 1944, daughter of Josefa de Gannon Martinez.

MRS. ACACIA O. RICKARD, November 18, 1944, daughter of Don Gaspar Orena.

MISS MARIA TRUSSELL, December 4, 1944, daughter of Captain Trussell.

MR. STEVEN T. VALENZUELA, June 26, 1942, former owner of El Cuartel.

MRS. A. L. MURPHY VHAY, December 1, 1944, restorer of the Gonzales adobe.

MRS. A. J. VERHELLE, June 25, 1942, granddaughter of William Benjamin Foxen.

MR. ALBERT W. WEEKLY, June 15, 1942, one time owner of the Caneda adobe.

MR. AND MRS. ELMER WHITAKER, July 5, 1942, owners of the Caneda adobe.

MR. AND MRS. ERNEST WICKENDEN, August 12, 1942. Mrs. Wickenden, granddaughter of Benjamin Foxen. Mr. Wickenden, son of Frederick Wickenden.

MR. J. R. WICKENDEN, September 27, 1944, son of Frederick Wickenden and owner of Wickenden adobe.

MRS. JAMES G. WILLIAMS, July 8, 1942, occupant of the Daniel Hill adobe at Goleta.